Contents

Creepy Crafty
Halloween

Compiled by Dawn Anderson

Martingale
& C O M P A N Y

BOTHELL, WASHINGTON

Credits

President . . . . Nancy J. Martin
CEO . . . . Daniel J. Martin
Publisher . . . . Jane Hamada
Editorial Director . . . . Mary V. Green
Editorial Project Manager . . . . Tina Cook
Technical Editor . . . . Dawn Anderson
Copy Editor . . . . Candie Frankel
Design and Production Manager . . . . Stan Green
Illustrator . . . . Laurel Strand
Photographer . . . . Brent Kane
Cover and Text Designer . . . . Rohani Design

Library of Congress Cataloging-in-Publication Data

Anderson, Dawn M.
   Creepy crafty Halloween / compiled by Dawn
   Anderson.
     p. cm.
   ISBN 1-56477-306-X
     1. Halloween decorations. 2. Handicraft. I. Title.

TT900.H32 A53 2000
745.594'1—dc21   00-037248

Creepy Crafty Halloween © Martingale & Company
Martingale & Company
PO Box 118
Bothell, WA 98041-0118 USA
www.patchwork.com

All rubber stamps used in this book have trademark
registration with the US Copyright Office.

Party Swirl Stamp © All Night Media

MISSION STATEMENT

*We are dedicated to providing quality products
and service by working together to inspire creativity
and to enrich the lives we touch.*

Printed in Hong Kong
05 04 03 02 01 00   6 5 4 3 2 1

The information in this book is presented in good faith,
but no warranty is given nor results guaranteed. Since
Martingale & Company has no control over choice of mate-
rials or procedures, the company assumes no responsibility
for the use of this information.

Introduction

Celebrating Halloween is as thrilling for adults as it is for children. Even if you don't dress in costume, you can enjoy the holiday by making some of the fabulous decorations found in this book.

Welcome trick-or-treaters to your home with a whimsical black cat stitched on a Halloween banner or painted on a floor cloth. Or, greet your guests with a spectacular glowing pumpkin. For a twist on the traditional jack-o'-lantern, try your hand at carving a one-of-a-kind witch pumpkin, using special tools to create the intricate design.

If you plan to host a party, start by creating one of the clever party invitations on pages 6–11. Your guests will be delighted to find one of these invitations waiting for them in the mail. Dazzle your party-goers with paper lanterns, glowing with images of black cats, pumpkins, and haunted houses. Or create etched glass luminaries of skeletons and ghosts, using clear glass vases and the stencils found in this book.

Serve your guests a batch of holiday goodies on an enchanting glass pedestal cake plate featuring a coordinating glass dome cover. The spiderweb plate design and ghost dome are painted with glass paints and baked in your home oven for a permanent finish. Your guests will also enjoy receiving a handmade party favor. Choose from three different styles of favors, including a small metal tin dressed as a pumpkin, or a vellum ghost bag. You may want to create some special table linens for the party as well. If you enjoy sewing, try the appliquéd pumpkin table runner. For a simple no-sew project, you can photo-transfer Halloween images onto ready-made linen place mats.

In addition to party-related accessories, this book includes many other decorations so charming, you may want to make them just for yourself. Projects include a paper-pieced scarecrow wall hanging, a trio of rug-hooked wall hangings, a collection of comical pumpkin heads, and a friendly witch doll with a companion black cat.

The projects in this book cover a variety of skill levels and craft mediums. You're sure to find several projects suitable for your next Halloween decorating adventure.

come to a party

it's a
Hall**o**ween
party

You're invited
to a

Masquerade
Party

at
the Baker House

7 PM
October 31

Costume
required

You are
invited to a
Halloween party
at

Emma and

Cooper's

house

Party Invitations

Announce your Halloween party with one of these special invitations. To produce the lettering, use rubber stamps or a computer and printer, or simply write the message yourself using a decorative marker or calligraphy pen.

TIP ▶ To make a crisp fold in card stock (or any stiff or thick paper), score it first. Lay the card stock on a flat surface, and align a ruler on the desired fold line. Drag a bone folder along the ruler edge, as you would a pencil, to make a light impression. If you don't have a bone folder, you can substitute the back (dull) edge of a table knife. Now simply fold along the scored line.

Tasseled Book Invitation

by Dave Brethauer

Materials

2 sheets celery ribbed text-weight paper, 8½" x 11"
1 sheet celery ribbed cover weight paper, 8½" x 11"
Canson watercolor paper, 140 lb. cold press
1¾" gold tassel on a cord
⅝ yard gold cording
Ruler
Pencil
Computer and printer
Garamouche font (optional)
Craft knife and self-healing mat
Bone folder
Double-coated tape
4 Halloween rubber stamps from Rubbermoon (Tree, DB4924J; Lady with Pumpkins, JC834H; Skeleton, JC449D; Wizard, JC445D)

Black waterproof ink pad (such as Printworks Outliners Pad)
Paintbrushes, size 6 round
Winsor & Newton Cotman watercolors: cadmium yellow, permanent rose, cobalt blue

TIP ▶ To work out your technique, practice mixing the watercolors and painting stamped images before you make your card.

Instructions

1. Lay the 3 celery papers flat. Using a ruler and pencil, lightly draft a solid line crosswise to divide each sheet in half. Draft a dashed line lengthwise to divide each sheet in quarters.

Using a computer, enter the invitation text so that it will print in the appropriate quadrants as shown. Use any desired font (I used Garamouche). Print on 2 sheets of text-weight paper.

8½" x 11" text weight paper
Pages 1 and 8 (top)
Pages 2 and 3 (bottom)

8½" x 11" text weight paper
Pages 4 and 5 (top)
Pages 6 and 7 (bottom)

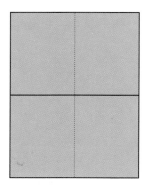

8½" x 11" cover weight paper

2. Cut each sheet on the solid lines using a craft knife. Score and fold the remaining pieces on the dashed lines (see Tip on page 7).

3. Tape a half sheet of cover weight paper to the back side of pages 1 and 8, using double-coated tape. Align the tassel along the fold of the cover weight side of the paper, so the tassel dangles 3" beyond the lower edge. Tape in place along the fold.

Pages 1 and 8

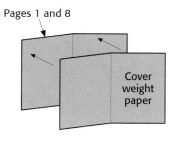

Cover weight paper

4. Tape the back of page 2 to the back of page 1, leaving page 3 free.

5. Tape the left side of the remaining half-sheet of cover weight paper to the back of page 3.

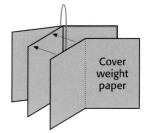

Cover weight paper

6. Tape pages 4 and 5 on top of the cover weight paper.

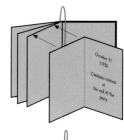

We'll play games and dance to ghoulish music

7. Tape page 6 to the back of page 5, leaving page 7 free.

8. Tape page 7 to the back of page 8.

9. Wrap the gold cord around the outer spine of the card and along the center fold in the center of the book. Knot both cord ends together at the lower edge of the card. Tie a knot 1" from the end of each cord, then fray the cord below the knot.

10. Stamp 4 Halloween images onto watercolor paper, using black waterproof ink. Mix cadmium yellow and permanent rose paints to

create a warm orange color. Use the paint to create a textured wash around the images. Add more rose for a deeper orange and more yellow for lighter orange. Mix a small amount of cobalt blue and cadmium

yellow to make green. Paint green accents where desired.

11. Let the watercolor images dry. Cut them out and tape them to the book pages at different angles, opposite the text pages.

Pumpkin Spinner Card

by Dave Brethauer

Materials

1 sheet orange card stock, 8½" x 11"
1 sheet olive card stock, 8½" x 11"
Computer and printer
Garamouche font (optional)
Fiskars circle cutter
Prismacolor colored pencil, PC 1032 pumpkin
 orange
Scissors
Black marking pen
³⁄₁₆" Anywhere hole punch
Black ³⁄₁₆" eyelet and eyelet setter tool
Hammer

Instructions

1. Using a computer, enter the text "it's a Halloween party" but substitute a space for the "o" in "Halloween." Use any desired font (I used Garamouche). Print the text onto orange card stock.

2. Position the circle cutter on the printed orange card stock with the missing "o" at the center. Cut out a circle ¾" beyond the edge of the wording; my orange circle is 5" in diameter.

3. Trim the circle with scissors as indicated by the dashed line in the illustration below, so the invitation is pumpkin-shaped rather than perfectly round. Use the orange colored pencil to draw in and shade the pumpkin ridges.

4. Cut a circle from the olive card stock ⅛" larger in diameter than the orange circle. Write the party details (place, date, time, etc.) around the edge of the circle with a black marking pen.

5. Center the orange pumpkin on the olive circle, right sides up. Punch a ³⁄₁₆" hole through the center of both pieces, using the Anywhere hole punch. Insert the eyelet through both holes. Turn the project over. Insert the eyelet setter tool into the back of the eyelet and tap with a hammer to set the eyelet. Spin the orange circle around to read the message on the olive circle.

Vellum Overlay Invitation

by Dave Brethauer

Materials

1 sheet handmade olive card stock, 8½" x 11"
1 sheet orange vellum, 8½" x 11"
1 sheet celery card stock, 8½" x 11"
Scrap of ivory linen card stock
Ruler
Pencil
Bone folder
Computer and printer
Garamouche font (optional)
Craft knife and self-healing cutting mat
³⁄₁₆" Anywhere hole punch
Celery green ³⁄₁₆" eyelet and eyelet setter tool
Hammer
Pumpkin girl rubber stamp from Rubbermoon, JC235B
Fawn Impress ink pad
Light brown marker
Scissors
Double-coated tape

TIP ▶ Vellum prints best on laser printers. If your computer printer is not a laser printer, try printing your invitation text on copier paper and then photocopying the text onto vellum.

Instructions

1. Using a ruler and pencil, lightly draft 2 lines crosswise on the olive card stock, dividing it in thirds. Score and fold both lines (see Tip on page 7). Set aside.

2. Using a computer, enter your invitation text (place, date, time, etc.) in any desired font (I used Garamouche). Print the text onto orange vellum, centering it. Trim the orange vellum to 2½" x 7½" so the text is centered.

3. Cut a 3" x 8" rectangle from the celery card stock. Center the orange vellum on it, then center both pieces on the middle olive panel. Punch a ³⁄₁₆" hole through all three layers about ¾" from the upper edge. Insert the eyelet through the holes. Turn the project over. Insert the eyelet setter tool into the back of the eyelet and tap with a hammer to set the eyelet.

4. Stamp the pumpkin girl image onto ivory linen card stock using the Fawn Impress ink pad. Let dry, then shade with a light brown marker. Cut out the image ⅛" outside the stamped area. Tape it to the bottom of the orange vellum sheet.

Witch Hat Invitation

by Kathryn Perkins

Instructions

1. Trace or photocopy the witch hat invitation pattern on page 73. Cut out the paper pattern. Lay the card stock black side down, set the pattern on top, and trace the outline. Cut out the card. Score the card on the dashed line (see Tip on page 7).
2. Lay the card flat, black side up. On the hat portion (front of card), stamp "You're Invited" using pigment ink. Stamp two stars above and two stars below the message. Sprinkle gold sparkle embossing powder on the wet ink, and shake off the excess. Heat with a heating tool to melt the powder.
3. Turn the card over, white side up. Stamp the "Party Swirl" and invitation stamps on the triangular portion (inside of card), using black dye ink.
4. Write your invitation information in the blanks using the black marking pen. Fold the card on the scored line.

Materials

1 sheet glossy black card stock (reverses to matte white), 8½" x 11"

Pencil

Craft knife and self-healing cutting mat

Ruler

Bone folder

"You're Invited" rubber stamp from Graphistamp 5900-S

Star rubber stamp from PSX (A262)

Pigment ink for embossing

Gold sparkle embossing powder

Heating tool

"Party Swirl" rubber stamp from All Night Media 809G

Invitation rubber stamp from Impress B4538

Black dye ink pad

Black fine-point marking pen

Halloween Cat Banner

by Sheila Haynes Rauen

This banner is constructed from light-weight nylon fabric using the reversible appliqué technique. When completed, it is one layer in thickness yet can be viewed from both sides. It can be hung outdoors from a banner pole or displayed indoors in a picture window to create a stained glass look. If you choose to make an outdoor banner, be sure to use fade-resistant fabric and thread.

Materials

Fade-resistant nylon flag bunting, 60" wide:
    1 yard royal blue
    ½ yard yellow
    ½ yard black
    ¼ yard orange
    ¼ yard white
Access to a photocopier
Transparent tape
Ruler
Pencil
Black felt-tip marking pen
Chalk pencils, light and dark colors
Sewing machine with zigzag stitch
Fusible thread for bobbin
Polyester thread in the fabric colors
General sewing tools
Iron, ironing board, and press cloth
Tear-away water-soluble stabilizer
Fiskars appliqué scissors

APPLIQUÉ TIP ▶ Test your stitching on scraps of the banner fabric before working on the final project. This will allow you to adjust your sewing machine tension settings.

• To appliqué around a corner, stop with the needle in the down position at the outside edge of the zigzag stitch. Lift the presser foot, pivot, lower the foot, and continue stitching down the adjacent side.

• On tight curves, take a few stitches, ending with the needle in the down position on the outside edge of the curve. Turn the fabric slightly and take a few more stitches. Continue in this manner until the curve is completely stitched.

Instructions

1. Enlarge the Halloween cat banner pattern on page 74 on a photocopier. Tape the photocopies together as necessary to complete the pattern. Darken all the lines using a black felt-tip marking pen.

2. Lay the royal blue background fabric on the pattern. Using a contrasting chalk pencil, mark all the pattern outlines to aid in positioning the appliqués; set the blue fabric aside. Lay the yellow fabric on the pattern. Trace the moon outline, including the extension at the top edge. Also trace the yellow eyes. Repeat this step to trace 1 cat, 2 hats, 2 hatbands, and 3 stars, each on the appropriate color fabric. Do not cut out the pieces yet.

3. Fill a sewing machine bobbin with fusible thread. Thread the upper machine with yellow thread. Stitch the yellow fabric along the moon's curved edge as marked. Cut out the moon just outside this edgestitching; work carefully to avoid cutting into the stitching.

4. Lay the blue background fabric marked side up. Position the yellow moon on it and fuse in place, following the fusible thread manufacturer's instructions. Make sure the iron setting isn't too hot as this may melt the nylon fabric; use a thin press cloth or piece of muslin to protect the fabric.

5. On the underside, back the fused area with tear-away water-soluble stabilizer; pin from the "right" side. Change to yellow bobbin thread to match the thread in the top of the machine. Set the machine for medium-width, fairly close zigzag stitches (but not satin stitch). From the right side, stitch around the curved edge of the moon through both layers.

6. Set the zigzag stitch slightly wider than before but keep the same stitch length. On the underside, tear away the stabilizer, then zigzag around the moon's curved edge over the previous stitches.

Color Plan

7. Trim away the blue fabric from behind the moon shape, using the appliqué scissors.

8. Repeat steps 3–6 to prepare, fuse, and sew the black cat appliqué; use the appropriate threads and break off the stitching where the hats will be appliquéd later. Trim away the blue fabric from behind the cat.

9. Appliqué the orange hats in place, breaking the stitching where the hatbands will be applied. Carefully trim away the blue, black, and yellow fabrics from behind the orange hats.

10. Appliqué the black hatbands in place. Trim away the orange fabric from behind the hatbands. Create the buckles by zigzag-stitching a rectangle with yellow thread on the center of each hatband on both sides of the banner, as shown in the photo on page 13.

11. Appliqué the stars in place. Trim away the blue fabric from behind the stars.

12. Appliqué the yellow eyes in place, using white thread, but do not trim behind the eyes yet. Draw a curved line on each yellow eye indicating the lower edge of the black iris. Zigzag on the marked line with black thread on both sides of the banner. On the right side, carefully trim away the upper yellow area to reveal the black iris. On the underside, trim away the lower black area to reveal the yellow eye. You should now have the proper eye colors on both sides of the banner.

13. Zigzag-stitch the cat's nose, mouth, and whiskers on both sides of the banner with white thread. You may wish to use a slightly narrower stitch width for these details.

14. Fold each side edge of the banner ½" to the underside; press. Fold and press again, then stitch close to the first fold. You can use a single-color thread to stitch around the banner, or you can change the thread colors to match the fabrics. Hem the bottom edge in the same way. Fold the top edge under ½", fold along the casing line, and pin. Stitch along the first fold to complete the casing.

Painted Floor Cloth

by Sheila Haynes Rauen

Greet your Halloween party guests with a painted floor cloth picturing a whimsical black cat and devil-costumed bird. Use the floor cloth on a sheltered porch outdoors or in your front entryway. (A nonskid rug mat underneath prevents slipping.) The paint used for this project is a water-based enamel that has a gloss finish. It is recommended that you practice using the paints and try different brushstroke techniques on scrap canvas before painting the actual floor cloth canvas. Most of the paint colors were used directly from the can. Stir the paints well before using, clean your brushes often to avoid paint build-up, and follow the manufacturer's instructions for drying and curing times. Once the paint and sealer coats have cured, the floor cloth can be wiped clean with mild soap and water.

Color Plan

TIPS ▶ • Create glazes by mixing paints with water.

• When doing line work for details, always thin paints with water and test for proper coverage over background colors.

• To mix your own paint colors, always begin with the lighter color. Add small amounts of the darker color until the desired value is reached.

• Always paint the background of the picture first, then work toward the foreground. Make sure the edges of the canvas are thoroughly painted and sealed with the clear finish coating.

• You can prime heavy artist's canvas on each side with gesso as a substitute for Kunin Kreative Kanvas or for preprimed floor canvas. Apply the gesso to each side, then cut the canvas to size. You must allow for shrinkage when using unprimed canvas. After cutting the canvas to size, make sure all the edges are coated with gesso.

Materials

Kunin Kreative Kanvas rectangle rug, 28" x 36", or preprimed floor cloth canvas cut to the desired size

Gesso

Access to a photocopier

Deka Sign Enamel (water-based) in the following colors: blue, black, primrose yellow, orange, medium green, white, bright red

Deka Clear Coat (for protective finish coats)

Paper or drop cloth to protect your work surface (freezer paper with the shiny side up works well)

2" brush (for gesso application)

1" wash brush (for borders and larger areas of color)

Shader brush, size 12

Liner brush

Paint remover tool (Loew Cornell)

Card stock for star and candy corn templates

Black marking pen

Chalk pencil

Graphite paper (to transfer pattern)

Nonskid rug mat

Instructions

1. Protect your work surface with paper or a drop cloth. Brush an even coat of gesso on one side of the precut floor cloth canvas. Allow gesso to dry thoroughly. Repeat to coat the reverse side. Let dry several hours.

2. To mark the border, draft a line 3" in from each edge of the canvas all around with the chalk pencil. Overlap the lines to create a "box" in each corner of the border.

3. Enlarge the floor cloth pattern on page 76 on a photocopier. Tape the photocopies together as necessary to complete the pattern. Transfer the basic design outlines to the canvas, within the border lines, using graphite paper. Don't transfer all of the details on the cat yet; you will transfer these later, after applying the black background color. Trace the stars, candy corn, and leaves onto card stock and cut out to make templates. Use the templates to mark these shapes on the floor cloth, referring to the color plan on page 16 as a guide.

4. Using the 1" brush, paint the corner squares and the background sky area blue. Paint carefully around the star and moon shapes.

5. Paint the lower background area medium green. Paint the border and the cat black.

6. Paint the bird, moon, cat's eyes, and jack-o'-lantern's facial details yellow. Paint the pumpkin, bird's beak and legs, and leaves orange. Paint the stars, lower part of the bird's eyes, and candy corn white. Paint yellow and orange bands of color on the candy corn after the white basecoat dries.

7. Paint the devil mask, horns, and pitchfork red. Paint the upper part of the bird's eyes, shadows in the jack-o'-lantern face, and upper part of cat's eyes black.

8. Draw the face, leg, and tail details on the cat, using a chalk pencil. Dilute a small amount of white paint with water, and paint the details using the liner brush.

9. Draw details on the bird's body and wings, using a chalk pencil. Dilute a small amount of red paint with water, and paint the details using the liner brush.

10. Mix a dark orange glaze by adding red paint to orange paint and water. Shade the lower beak and legs of the bird with the glaze. Using the same glaze, add some shading to the jack-o'-lantern to make pumpkin ridges as shown in the photo on page 15. Also use some of this glaze on the leaves. After applying the glaze to the leaves, use the paint remover tool to "draw" veins on the leaves while the glaze is still wet.

11. Mix a light orange glaze for the pumpkin by adding orange paint to white paint and water. Paint the glaze on the pumpkin, using the photo on page 15 as a guide.

12. Mix a light green glaze for the grass by adding medium green paint to white paint and water. Working on a small area at a time, paint the lighter green glaze over the darker green. While the glaze is still wet, pull upward in random strokes with the paint remover tool to create blades of grass. Overlap the strokes onto the cat, pumpkin, and leaves.

13. Allow the paint to dry thoroughly. Paint a band of black paint approximately 1" wide around the back edge of the floor cloth to finish.

14. Following the manufacturer's instructions, apply 3 coats of Clear Coat to the floor cloth. Allow to cure for 1 week before using. Cut a nonskid mat 1" smaller than the floor cloth all around and place underneath before using. Use on bare floors only.

Carved Witch Pumpkin

by Pumpkin Masters, America's Pumpkin Carving Company

L et the golden glow of this witch pumpkin welcome your party guests or trick-or-treaters. Ordinary jack-o'-lanterns can be carved with tools you have at home, but to cut the intricate design shown here or to make a detailed design of your own, you will need a few specially designed pumpkin carving tools. See sources on page 111.

Materials

Pumpkin
Pumpkin Masters tools and supplies:
    Lid-Cutter Saw
    Scraper Scoop
    Poker
    Starter Saw
    Candle Holder
    Candle
Newspapers
Dull pencil
Tracing paper
Tape
Scissors

Instructions

1. Cover your work surface with newspapers. Draw a lid on the top of your pumpkin, using the pencil. Draw a "tooth" at the back of the lid to use as a guide for replacing the lid. Cut carefully along the marked lines with the Lid-Cutter Saw, angling the blade toward the center of the pumpkin to create a ledge to support the lid.
2. Clean out the pumpkin seeds using the Scraper Scoop. Scrape the inner pulp away from the area you plan to carve until the pumpkin wall is about 1" thick.
3. Trace the witch pumpkin pattern on page 75 onto tracing paper. Trim the pattern ½" from the outer edge of the design. Tape the pattern to your pumpkin, creasing the paper at the dashed lines for a smooth fit. Tape down the creased sections so they lie flat.
4. Poke holes along the pattern design lines, about ⅛" apart, using the tip of the Poker. Note that all yellow colored areas of the pattern denote areas of the pumpkin to be removed. When all the lines are transferred, remove the pattern. If the design is hard to see, connect the dots with a dull pencil.
5. Hold the pumpkin in your lap. Starting with the cat, grasp the Starter Saw like a pencil and insert it into the pumpkin on the dotted design line. Saw steadily, dot-to-dot, at a 90-degree angle to the pumpkin, using gentle pressure. At the corners, remove the saw and then reinsert it. Next, saw the broom bristles, the witch, and the broom handle. Saw the outer circle last. To protect the delicate broom handle, remove the large cutout area in sections. Push out the cut pieces with your finger, not the saw blade.
6. Insert the candle into the Candle Holder. Attach the Candle Holder to the bottom of your pumpkin. Remove the lid, and tilt the pumpkin to light the candle. Replace the lid. The candle smoke will blacken a spot under the lid. Use the Lid-Cutter Saw to cut a chimney hole at this spot to vent the smoke and heat.

Witch Doll with Cat

by Ruth Landis

This friendly witch, with her black cat spook, stands guard over Halloween goodies. She has bendable arms, and wooden dowel legs hold her upright. Her costume is made from unmatched cotton print fabrics for a whimsical look. Substitute a variety of black fabrics for a more traditional approach.

Materials

42"-wide cotton fabrics:

- ⅜ yard black for cat, hat, and hair
- ½ yard purple print for jumper, waistband, and straps
- ¼ yard fleshtone for head, arms, and neck
- ¼ yard green print for boots
- ¼ yard black-and-tan check for body and sleeves
- ⅛ yard black-and-white striped for one leg
- ⅛ yard black-and-blue striped for one leg
- ⅛ yard purple for hair
- Scrap for hat trim
- Scrap for jumper patch

¼ yard low-loft cotton batting or craft felt for body and neck

Polyester fiberfill

4 seed beads for eyes

Powder blush and cotton swab

Wire, 16–18 gauge

Wooden dowel, ½" diameter

Black buttonhole twist

8 orange buttons, ⅜" diameter

Heavy-duty thread

4" x 6" oval wood plaque

Glitter spray

Paper for patterns

Pencil

Water-soluble marking pen

Sewing machine

General sewing tools

Iron and ironing board

Thread to match fabrics

Beading needle

Fine-line permanent marking pens, such as Sakura Micron Pigma pens, .01 nib size, in desired colors

Rotary cutter with pinking blade, or pinking shears (optional)

Wire cutter

Ruler

Embroidery needle (for buttonhole twist)

Long doll needle

Drill with ½" bit

Saw

> **TIP ▶** Stuff the witch and cat firmly for a professional appearance. Use bamboo skewers, dowels, and toothpicks of various sizes to push the stuffing into small or hard-to-reach areas.

Cut the Fabrics

1. Trace or photocopy the 14 witch and cat patterns on pages 77–80. Use the patterns to cut the following pieces:

From the black fabric, cut:
- 2 cats
- 1 hat top
- 2 hat brims

From the purple print, cut:
- 1 rectangle, 10" x 20", for the jumper skirt
- 1 jumper waistband
- 2 jumper straps

From the fleshtone fabric, cut:
    2 head fronts
    1 head back
    2 necks
    2 arms
From the black-and-tan check, cut:
    2 bodies
    2 sleeves
From the green print, cut:
    2 boots
From each striped fabric, cut:
    1 leg
From the scraps, cut:
    1 jumper patch
    1 rectangle, 1¾" x 5", for hat trim
From the batting or craft felt, cut:
    2 bodies
    2 necks

2. Transfer the pattern markings to the fabric pieces as indicated on the patterns. Use a water-soluble pen to transfer the facial details.

> **TIP ▶** To mark the facial details easily, use this tracing technique: Hold the cut fabric piece right side up against a window or on a light box. Slip the pattern underneath with the edges matching. Trace the facial features onto the right side of the fabric.

Note: Sew all pieces with a ¼" seam allowance, unless otherwise noted.

Make the Head

1. Pin 1 head front to the head back, right sides together, matching dots. Sew from A to B. Sew the remaining head front to the other edge of the head back in the same manner. Pin the head fronts right sides together, matching dots. Sew from C to B. Trim and clip seam allowances as necessary. Turn the head right side out.

2. Fold the raw neck edge ¼" to the inside. Stuff the head with polyester fiberfill, taking special care to make the nose extra-firm.

3. Sew a seed bead to the witch's face at each eye dot, using a beading needle.

4. Use a Pigma pen to lightly dot the mouth. Follow the transfer marks, and slowly and carefully fill in the dots with more color until the desired effect is achieved. I used blue to outline the mouth and filled it in with other colors to match the clothing. Allow the marks to dry. Wipe away any remaining transfer marks.

5. Use blue and brown Pigma pens to go over the eyebrows with short, light strokes. Continue adding strokes until the desired effect is achieved. Use a blue Pigma pen to draw in the eyes, eyelids, and eyelashes.

6. Apply powder blush lightly to cheeks with your finger or a cotton swab. Add more color, if needed.

7. Cut ¼" x 18" strips from the black and purple fabrics, using a rotary cutter or scissors. A pinking blade or pinking shears provides an interesting effect. The number of strips needed will depend on the desired effect. Hand stitch the strips to the doll's head; trim length if needed and style the hair. Set aside.

Make the Body Pieces

1. Pin each fabric body and neck piece, right side up, to a corresponding batting or craft felt piece. Machine-baste ⅛" from the raw edges all around.

2. Pin each padded neck to a padded body, right sides together, stitch together. Pin the body/neck pieces right sides together, and stitch around the outer edges, leaving the lower edge open for the legs. Trim and clip the seam allowances.

3. Turn the body right side out. Fold the lower edge to the inside along the marked fold line. Firmly stuff the body with polyester fiberfill to the fill line.

4. Fold each arm in half, right side in. Stitch the edges together, leaving the short, straight end open. Trim and clip the seam allowances; turn right side out. Stuff each hand lightly. Stitch on the dashed lines to create fingers.

5. Cut a piece of wire 7½" long, using the wire cutter. Bend the wire back on itself by ½" at each end. Insert the wire into the arm, so one end lodges in a central finger and the other end is at the shoulder. Stuff the hand and arm firmly, packing the fiberfill around the wire. Turn the raw edge ¼" to the inside and hand stitch closed, concealing the wire inside. Repeat for the other arm.

6. Pin each leg to the top of a boot, right sides together; stitch. Press the seam allowances toward the legs. Topstitch the seam allowances on the right side.

7. Fold each leg/boot in half lengthwise, right side in; pin. Stitch the long edge and boot toe together, but leave the boot heel and opposite leg end open. Trim the points and clip the inner corners. Turn right side out. Stuff the boot toe with polyester fiberfill.

8. Cut the dowel to make two 12"-long pieces. Turn the heel opening of each boot ¼" to the inside. Push a dowel through the opening and up the leg until just ½" of the dowel extends below the heel. Glue the heel to the dowel. Push fiberfill down the leg to fill in the ankle; fiberfill is not needed in the leg. Gather the leg fabric around the top of the dowel and glue in place.

9. Thread embroidery needle with black buttonhole twist. Using the dots as a placement guide, "sew" laces onto the boots. Tie each lace in a bow, and trim off the excess. Set aside all the body pieces.

Make the Jumper

1. Cut a zigzag pattern (to match the sleeves) along a 20" edge of the jumper skirt rectangle. On the opposite edge, hand-sew 2 rows of long gathering stitches ⅛" and ¼" from the edge. Fold the jumper waistband in half lengthwise, wrong side in; press. Pull the gathering threads, adjusting the skirt to fit the waistband. Pin the waistband to the gathered skirt edge, right sides together, and stitch. Trim the seam allowances to ⅛". Zigzag over the seam allowance.

2. Fold the skirt in half, right side in, matching the edges and waistband seam. Stitch from the waistband to the lower edge. Turn right side out; press.

3. Fold each jumper strap in half lengthwise, right side in. Stitch the long raw edges together. Turn right side out. Press.

4. Position the strap ends inside the waistband, matching the X's, and hand stitch together. Sew buttons to the right side of the front waistband over the X's. Hand stitch the patch to the front of the jumper, between the waistband and hem. Set the jumper aside.

Make the Hat

1. Fold the hat top in half, right side in; pin. Sew long raw edges together. Trim point. Turn right side out. Turn the lower edge ⅜" to the inside.

2. Pin the brim pieces right sides together. Sew all around, leaving an opening at one short end (see pattern). Trim and clip seam allowances. Turn right side out. Press.

3. Fold the hat trim strip in half lengthwise, right side in; pin. Stitch the long edges together. Turn right side out. Fold the open edges to the inside.

4. Wrap the brim around the base of the hat top, overlapping the ends to fit. Slipstitch the brim to the lower folded edge of the hat top. Hand-stitch the brim ends together.

5. Wrap the trim around the hat, butting the ends at the hat seam line; hand stitch in place. Position 4 buttons evenly around the trim; stitch in place. Set the hat aside.

Make the Cat

1. Pin the cat pieces right sides together. Stitch ⅛" from the raw curved edges all around; leave the lower edge open.

2. Trim and clip the seam allowance. Turn the cat right side out. Stuff firmly with polyester fiberfill.

3. Hand-sew long gathering stitches ⅜" from the lower edge all around. Push the raw edges to the inside, and pull the thread to close the opening. Knot and clip the thread.

4. Sew a seed bead to each eye dot on the cat's face. For whiskers, thread the needle with black thread, even up the ends, and tie a knot 1½" from the ends. Insert the needle into the cat's face at an X and pull out at the adjacent X. Slightly tighten the thread, then make an overhand knot close to the face. Clip the excess thread 1½" from the knot. Repeat on the other side. Set the cat aside.

Complete the Assembly

1. Push the open end of the witch's head onto the neck stump. Adjust the fit and hand stitch securely.

2. Fold each sleeve in half, right side in. Stitch the curved edge, but leave the zigzag edge open. Trim and clip the seam allowances; turn right side out.

3. Cut a 36" length of heavy-duty thread. Thread both ends together onto a long needle. Put one arm into a sleeve so the tops touch and the sleeve seam is centered on the inside. Insert the needle from the seam side and draw it out at the X, but do not pull all the way through. Make a return stitch to the starting point, slip the needle through the loop, and pull snug. Push the needle back through to the other side.

4. Thread a button onto the needle. Hold both sleeve/arm pieces with the sleeve seam against the doll body and the shoulder X's aligned. Push the needle back through the sleeve/arm, the body, and the other sleeve/arm.

5. Thread the remaining button on the needle. Push the needle back through the second sleeve/arm, the body, the first sleeve/arm, and the first button. Continue to work the needle back and forth in this way for a firm hold. Knot and clip thread.

6. Push the top of each dowel leg into the lower end of the body for 3", with toes facing forward. Add more stuffing to the body around the legs for stability, if needed. Sew the opening closed around the legs.

7. Put the jumper and hat on the witch. If needed, glue or hand stitch to hold in place.

8. Drill two ½" holes 1½" apart in the middle of the wood plaque. Push the boot dowels into the holes and stand the witch upright. Bend the witch's fingers for a natural appearance; wrap the fingers of one hand around the cat's tail. Apply a light coat of glitter spray to set the face coloring and add a glow to the doll.

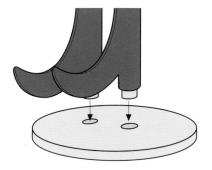

Crayon and Embroidery Wall Hanging

by Barri Gaudet

Create this delightful wall quilt with a few scraps of fabric, ordinary crayons, and some simple embroidery stitches. It features five Halloween quilt blocks. The blocks are separated by bright sashing strips and framed with a double border and binding. Hang the finished piece on a door or over a buffet for a splash of fun. The finished quilt measures about 16" x 16".

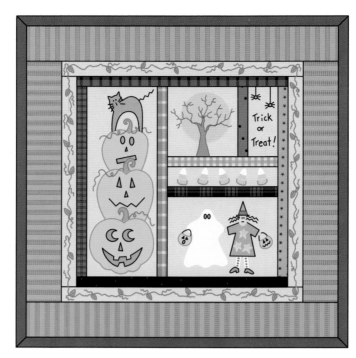

Quilt Plan

Materials

42"-wide cotton fabrics:

¼ yard tea-dyed muslin for the blocks and inner border

⅛ yard total scraps of different fabrics for the sashing

¼ yard for the outer border

⅛ yard for the binding

17" x 17" square for the backing

17" x 17" square of batting

DMC floss in the following colors:

921 orange

310 black

3820 yellow

433 brown

355 red

550 purple

758 peach

469 green

white

ecru

Sewing machine

General sewing tools

Thread to match fabrics

Iron and ironing board

Tape

Water-soluble marker

Crayola crayons in the following colors: red-orange, black, green, raw sienna, goldenrod, white, violet, and peach

Cut the Fabrics

Cut the following pieces.

From the muslin, cut:

1 rectangle, 4" x 10", for the Pumpkin Stack Block

1 square, 4" x 4", for the Tree Block

1 rectangle, 2" x 4", for the Trick or Treat! Block

1 rectangle, 1½" x 6", for the Candy Corn Block

1 rectangle, 4½" x 6", for the Ghost and Witch Block

2 strips, each 1¼" x 11", for the side inner borders

2 strips, each 1¼" x 12½", for the top and bottom inner borders

From the scraps for the sashing, cut:
    3 vertical sashing strips, each 1" x 10"
    2 horizontal sashing strips, each 1" x 11"
    2 horizontal sashing strips, each 1" x 6",
        for each side of the Candy Corn
        Block
    1 vertical sashing strip, 1" x 4", to go
        between the Tree Block and the
        Trick or Treat! Block
From the outer border fabric, cut:
    2 strips, each 2½" x 12½", for the side
        outer borders
    2 strips, each 2½" x 16½", for the top
        and bottom outer borders
From the binding fabric, cut:
    2 strips, each 1½" x 44"

Sew the Blocks Together

Note: Sew all pieces right sides together with a ¼" seam allowance.

1. Stitch the 1" x 4" sashing strip to one edge of the 4" muslin square for the Tree Block. Stitch the remaining 4" edge of the sashing strip to the muslin rectangle for the Trick or Treat! Block. Press the seam allowances toward the sashing strip. Lay the unit flat, right side up, with the Trick or Treat! Block on the right.
2. Stitch a 1" x 6" sashing strip to each long edge of the muslin rectangle for the Candy Corn Block.
3. Stitch the Candy Corn unit to the lower edge of the Tree/Trick or Treat! unit. Stitch the muslin rectangle for the Ghost and Witch Block to the lower edge of the Candy Corn unit. Press all the seam allowances toward the sashing strips. Stitch a 1" x 10" vertical sashing strip the right edge of the unit.
4. Stitch the remaining 1" x 10" vertical sashing strips to each long edge of the muslin rectangle for the Pumpkin Stack Block. Stitch the Pumpkin Stack unit to the left edge of

the pieced unit. Press the seam allowances toward the vertical sashing strips.
5. Stitch the horizontal sashing strips to the top and bottom edges of the pieced unit. Stitch the side inner borders to the side edges of the quilt top. Press the seam allowances toward the vertical sashing strips. Stitch the top and bottom inner borders to the top and bottom edges of the quilt top. Press the seam allowances toward the horizontal sashing strips.
6. Stitch the side outer borders to the side edges of the quilt top; press the seam allowances toward the outer border. Stitch the top and bottom outer border strips to the top and bottom edges of the quilt; press the seam allowances toward the outer border.

Color the Blocks

1. Trace or photocopy the quilt block and inner border patterns on pages 81–83. Tape the block designs to a window or place them on a light box, right side up. Position the quilt top over the block designs, right side up, taping if needed. Trace the designs onto the muslin blocks, using a water-soluble marker. Trace the inner border design onto the inner border.
2. Using the red-orange crayon, color the pumpkins in the Pumpkin Stack Block. Color the cat and the pumpkin faces black and the pumpkin stems green.
3. In the Tree Block, color the tree raw sienna and the moon goldenrod.
4. In the Trick or Treat! Block, color each of the spiders black.
5. In the Candy Corn Block, color each candy corn white at the top, goldenrod in the middle, and red-orange at the bottom.
6. In the Ghost and Witch Block, color the pumpkin baskets red-orange. Color the ghost and the witch's stockings white. Color the witch's dress, hat, shoes, the ghost's eyes, and the pumpkin basket eyes black. Color

the stars on the witch's dress goldenrod. Color the hatband violet. Color the witch's head and hands peach.

7. Color each of the leaves around the inner border green.

Embroider the Blocks

Note: Stitch with 2 strands of floss for all of the embroidery work.

1. In the Pumpkin Stack Block, backstitch around the pumpkins with orange floss. Backstitch the pumpkin vines and around the stems with green floss. Backstitch the pumpkin faces and the cat with black floss. Make black French knots for the cat eyes.

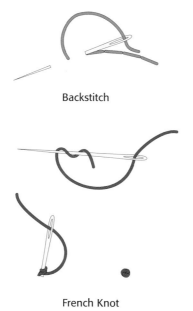

Backstitch

French Knot

2. In the Tree Block, backstitch around the moon with yellow floss and around the tree and tree branches with brown floss.

3. In the Trick or Treat! Block, backstitch the spiders and the lettering with black floss. Dot the "i" and complete the exclamation mark with French knots.

4. In the Candy Corn Block, backstitch around each candy corn, using white floss for the top, yellow floss for the middle, and orange floss for the bottom.

5. In the Ghost and Witch Block, backstitch around the ghost and the witch's stockings with ecru floss. Backstitch the stripes on the stockings with red floss. Backstitch the ghost's eyes, the witch's hat, hair, face, dress, and shoes, and the pumpkin basket faces and handles with black floss. Make black French knots for the witch's eyes. Backstitch around the pumpkin baskets with orange floss, the stars on the dress with yellow floss, the hatband with purple floss, and the witch's head and hands with peach floss.

6. Backstitch the vine and around the leaves on the inner border with green floss.

7. Remove all the water-soluble pen markings, following the manufacturer's instructions. If desired, heat-set the crayon colors by covering the design with white paper and pressing with a warm iron. Do not press any white areas, as this color lifts off.

Finish the Quilt

1. Place the backing fabric right side down and layer with batting. Place the quilt top right side up on the batting. Baste the layers together with safety pins, spacing them about 4" apart.

2. Stitch in the ditch between all blocks and sashing strips. Stitch in the ditch around all borders. Trim the edges of the batting and backing even with the quilt top, if necessary.

3. Measure the width of the quilt and subtract 1". Cut a strip of muslin to this length x 4½" wide, for a fabric sleeve. Fold in each short end ¼"; repeat, then stitch down along the first fold. Fold the strip in half lengthwise, wrong side in. Center the strip on the back top edge of the quilt so the raw edges are ¼"

apart; baste in place. Slipstitch the folded edge of the strip to the back of the quilt.

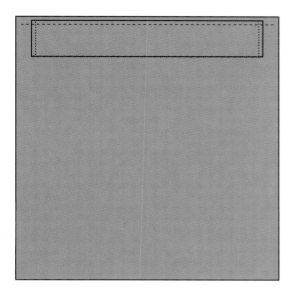

4. Join the binding strips in a diagonal seam; trim the seam allowance to ¼".

5. Press up ¼" on a long edge of the binding. Place the remaining long edge of the binding ¼" from the lower edge of the quilt top, right sides together. Stitch ¼" from the raw edge of the binding, starting 2" from the end; stop ½" from the corner. Backstitch and remove the quilt from the machine.

6. Fold the binding up at the corner, making a 45-degree angle. Then fold the binding straight down, with the fold ¼" from the edge of the quilt. The raw edges of the binding are now ¼" from and parallel to the raw edges on the next side.

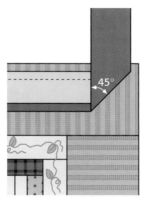
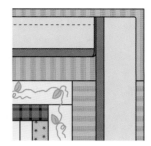

7. Begin stitching off the edge of the fold at the corner and continue until you are ½" from the next corner; backstitch and remove the quilt from the machine. Repeat step 6. Continue in the same manner around the remainder of the quilt. When you return to the starting point, turn under and overlap the ends, trimming off any excess.

8. Fold the binding onto the quilt back, mitering the corners. Pin in place, just covering the stitching line. Stitch in the ditch from the front, catching the binding on the back.

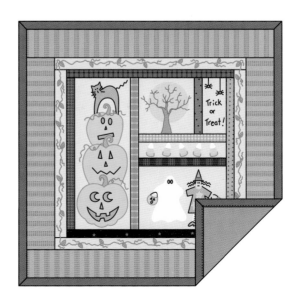

SPOOK
WANTED
INQUIRE WITHIN

Haunted Birdhouse

by Jenni Paige

Make this whimsical birdhouse to accent your table or buffet. The roof opens to reveal a tiny storage area, perfect for hiding Halloween treasures. This house started as a kit, made from cardboard. Follow the embellishing instructions given here or use your imagination to develop your own haunted creation.

Materials

Cardboard Birdhouse kit "B" from Calico Moon Handcrafts (See Sources Guide on page 111)
42"-wide cotton fabrics:
    3/8 yard for main house (turquoise)
    1/4 yard for roof (red-violet)
    1/4 yard for roof underside (purple)
    1/4 yard for attic walls and inside storage (teal)
    1/8 yard (or scraps) for doors (black)
    1/8 yard for door frames (red-violet)
    1/4 yard for house trim and chimney (red-orange)
    1/8 yard for shutters (gold/orange)
2 yards fusible web
1/4" wood dowel for perches
24 orange beads, size 5mm, for roof trim
Black Nymo beading thread
Green polymer modeling clay for the witch
Assorted motif buttons, such as bats, stars, moons, pumpkins, cat, frog, crow, and witch hat
Black curly doll hair
Black embroidery floss
2 miniature brooms
3 black beads, size 5mm, for witch brooms and hanging sign
Black craft wire, 18–20 gauge

1 package orange rickrack
1 wood bead, size 16mm, for the spider
Purple hemp twine
8 iridescent beads, for the spider
4 unpainted wood beads, size 25mm, for house "feet"
White Sakura Pen-Touch pen for the fake bricks
Black Pigma pen for the sign
Acrylic craft paint in the following colors:
    black-green, red, purple, and white
Aleene's regular or designer tacky glue
Aleene's Jewel It or Okay to Wash It glue
Iron and ironing board
Sewing shears
Ruler
Masking tape
Utility knife
Flat artist's paintbrush
Pencil
Beading needle
Liner brush
Jewelry pliers
Darning needle
Toothpick
Saw

Before you begin, read through all the instructions that come with the house kit, keeping in mind a few changes:
• Wood dowel perches were added, so this house does not have a door that opens in front. The front door piece in your kit will be the back of the house.
• Door holes are not punched out.
• Extra details, such as the shutters, trim, and chimney, were made using the scrap pieces of cardboard included with your house pieces. A similar weight cardboard may be substituted.

Construct the House

1. Apply fusible web to the wrong side of the main house fabric, covering a 13" x 22" area; follow the manufacturer's instructions for fusing and butt pieces of web together as necessary. Using the cardboard house pieces as patterns, cut out the Birdhouse Wall Outside #4, adding ¾" to all sides, and the Birdhouse Door Outside #5, adding 1" to all sides, from the fabric. Since the front of our house does not open, you can omit cutting fabric to cover the inside walls as directed in the kit.

2. Draw fake bricks onto the fabric pieces cut in step 1, if desired. Use a ruler to mark occasional dashed lines across the fabric, and fill in by hand for an uneven, more realistic look.

3. Apply fusible web to the wrong sides of the roof fabrics; use the pattern as a guide to size and butt pieces of web together as necessary. Cut 1 Roof Outside and 1 Roof Underside, using the kit's #7 Roof pattern. Cut 1 Roof Outside on the outer solid line and cut 1 Roof Underside on the inner solid line.

4. Apply fusible web to the wrong side of the fabric for the attic walls and inside storage area; cover a 9" x 30" area, butting pieces of web together as necessary. From the fabric, cut 1 piece using the kit's large pattern #6 Attic and 2 pieces using the small pattern #6 Attic. Also cut 1 piece using pattern #1 Tray and 1 piece using pattern #1 Inside Tray.

5. Fold in the sides of the tray so the brown side of the cardboard is on the inside; tape the corners at the top edge.

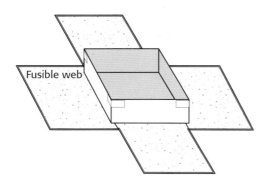

6. Turn the tray upside down. Put a small amount of tacky glue on the bottom of the tray; center the tray fabric, web side down, over the tray, and press to adhere.

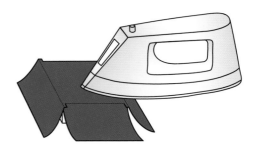

7. Fold the long sides up along the sides of the tray; press with the tip of your iron, folding excess fabric around the corners.

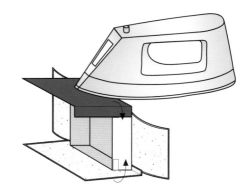

8. Press up the remaining sides.

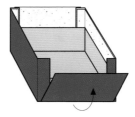

9. Apply a thin coat of glue on the inside bottom of the tray around the edges. Pull the side fabric to the inside, longer edges first, and glue to the bottom of the tray. Press the sides of the tray on the inside with the tip of the iron. Using a small amount of glue, secure the inside tray piece to the bottom of the tray. Make a second tray for the bottom of the birdhouse in the

same manner, omitting the inside tray piece. Use fabric that matches the birdhouse walls, if desired.

10. Glue a small cardboard shelf piece to each large shelf piece, aligning the straight edges; the larger piece goes on the bottom and will extend about ¼" beyond the small piece. Omit covering the shelves with fabric, since they are used for support only.

11. Remove the fusible web's paper backing from the Birdhouse Wall Outside #4. Place the corresponding cardboard piece on it, white side down. Press the 4 corners over the edge of the cardboard with the iron.

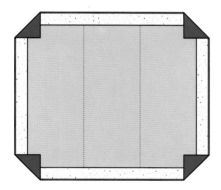

12. Turn the piece over and press on the fabric side. Turn the piece to the wrong side and fold the fabric over the edges, mitering the corners; press in place to secure. Cover the Birdhouse Door Outside #5 with its fabric in the same manner.

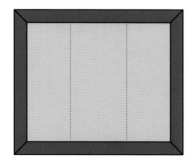

13. Cut the dowel to make three 4½"-long pieces. Paint 2" of the end of each dowel piece with black-green paint.

14. Trace the oval door and door frame patterns on page 84 onto the paper side of the fusible web 3 times each. Apply the web to the corresponding fabrics and cut out. Center the doors on the front of the house (the middle wall in the Birdhouse Wall Outside #4 piece you constructed in steps 11 and 12). Use a ruler if necessary to center the doors on the front of the house. Fuse lightly with a hot iron. Fuse the door frames around the doors.

15. Apply glue to 3 sides of the bottom tray. Wrap the bottom of the Birdhouse Wall Outside #4 around the tray, pressing it into the glue. Secure the sides to the open back temporarily with tape.

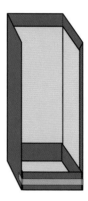

16. Apply glue to 3 sides of the attic tray, just on the lower half. Slide the tray into the 3 walls of the birdhouse from the top, pushing in only halfway. Be sure the upper edge is level. Secure temporarily with tape across the open back area. Allow to dry.

17. With the tip of a very sharp utility knife, gently cut an X, measuring about ¼" across, centered directly below each door frame. The bottom X will need to go through the tray, so you will have to do some carving with the tip of the craft knife from the inside of the tray to remove the excess cardboard. Ease a piece of dowel through each X, leaving 1" of the painted end sticking out for the perch.

18. Apply glue to the 3 straight edges of the 2 shelves and glue in place directly above the 2 upper perches on the inside of the house. Glue and tape the dowels to the shelves for extra stability. Secure the lower dowel with glue and tape to the floor of the bottom tray.

19. When the perches are dry and secure, glue the Birdhouse Door Outside #5 to the back of the house. This door will not open.

20. Tape the #6 cardboard pieces together on the brown side of the cardboard. Center the taped cardboard over the large piece of fabric for Attic #6; turn over and press. Turn over again, and clip inside corners. Press over the fabric at the corners. Press the lower and side fabric edges over, then the upper edges, mitering corners. Press the small Attic #6 pieces over the peaks on the inside.

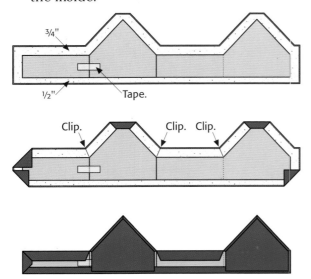

21. Apply glue to the top half of the upper tray and to 1 end of the attic piece. Wrap the attic piece around the tray, with the peaks of the attic at the front and back of the birdhouse. Butt the ends of the attic at 1 back corner of the birdhouse. Secure temporarily with tape.

22. Tape the 2 Roof #7 pieces together on the brown side of the cardboard, allowing ⅛" space between them. Fuse scraps of fabric around the edges of the concave curves of the roof. Center the roof white side down on the large piece of roof fabric. Turn over, and press. Turn over again. Clip around the curved edges. Press the edges over the cardboard. Center the small roof piece on the underside of the roof; press.

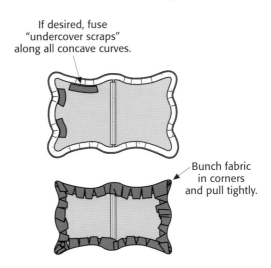

23. Thread a needle with beading thread and sew orange beads to the roof edges on each short side.

24. Apply glue to the top edges of half of the attic peaks and sides. Center roof on birdhouse; press in place.

Embellish the House

1. Cut 4 strips of cardboard, each ⅞" x 16⅞". Cut 4 strips of orange print fabric, each 3" x 17¼". Apply fusible web to the back of the fabric strips. Center the cardboard strips over the fabric and press. Press up the long edges over the cardboard. Glue the strips to the house to separate each story of the house as shown in the photo on page 30. Use masking tape to hold the strips in place while they dry.

2. Transfer the large and small shutter patterns on page 85 to thin cardboard; cut out to make 2 templates. Use the smaller template to cut 6 shutters from the leftover cardboard. Apply fusible web to the wrong side of the shutter fabric, covering a 4" x 12" area. Use the larger template to cut 6 shutters (reverse 3) from the fabric. Fuse the shutter fabric to the cardboard shutters; clip the fabric around the curves and press to the wrong side. Glue the shutters to the sides of each door on the house front, placing some of them slightly crooked, as if they were falling off.

3. Make a witch head from a small piece of green polymer clay. Knead the clay with your fingers until it is soft enough to form. Roll into a 1" ball and flatten into an oval. Pull out a long witchy nose and a long witchy chin. Use a toothpick to smooth the area between the nose and chin. Press the witch hat button onto the forehead to make an impression, then remove the button. Bake the witch in the oven for 10 to 12 minutes and allow to cool, following the clay manufacturer's instructions. Glue the hat button in place.

4. Glue beads to the witch for eyes; thread each bead onto a needle to help hold it while you put a small dot of glue on the back. Paint lips on the witch, using a liner brush and red paint.

5. Arrange doll hair behind the hat button. Glue the face, hair, and hat to the house, taping in place until dry.

6. Wrap embroidery floss around a broom in 3 locations to hold the bristles together, as shown in the photo on page 30. Glue a bead to the end of the handle for extra decoration. Glue a cat button to the broom handle. Carve a dent in the underside of the broom so you can balance it on the top perch. Glue the broom to the perch, taping until dry.

7. Wrap embroidery floss around the second broom in 2 locations, as shown in the photo. Glue a bead to the end of the handle. Glue the broom next to the witch head as shown.

8. Tie floss through pumpkin buttons and glue in place just above the house trim. Do the same with frog, crow, and star buttons.

9. Cut 1 chimney top, 1 chimney inside wall, 1 outside wall, and 2 chimney side walls from cardboard, using the templates on pages 84–85. Tape the chimney side, outside, and remaining side walls together in that order, allowing ⅛" space between them.

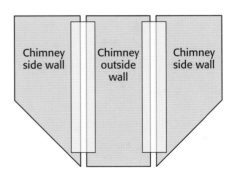

Apply fusible web to the wrong side of the chimney fabric, covering a 7" x 11" area; cut 1 chimney top piece, 1 chimney inside wall, and 1 chimney side and outside wall piece, using the patterns on page 84.

10. Fuse the chimney side and outside wall fabric piece to the corresponding taped cardboard pieces in the same manner as for the house pieces. Fuse the chimney inside wall fabric and the chimney top fabric to the corresponding pieces of cardboard.

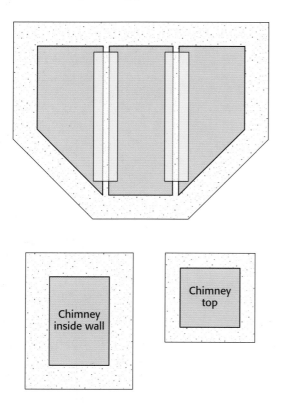

11. Cut several random lengths of wire. Thread each wire through a bat or star button and secure by bending the wire back on itself with jewelry pliers. Wrap each wire around a pencil to form spirals. Gather all the wire spirals into a nice bouquet and arrange with the taller pieces in back. Using a darning needle, punch a hole in the chimney top piece for each wire in your arrangement. Insert the wires through the cardboard, twist together on the underside, and secure with glue and tape. Place your bouquet upside down (glue side up) in a drinking glass to dry.

12. When the chimney top piece is dry, bend the outside chimney walls around the top piece; glue in place. Hold with tape until

dry. When dry, glue the chimney inside wall in place, then tape to hold until dry. When the chimney is dry, position it on the roof, in line with the house walls. Glue in place; tape until dry.

13. Glue orange rickrack around the attic trim. Glue a big star button to the attic. Make a little sign to hang on the lower door by fusing 2 small rectangles of orange fabric over a loop of embroidery floss. Cut a piece of muslin slightly smaller than the sign rectangle. Use the black Pigma pen to print "Spook Wanted, Inquire Within" on the muslin. Fuse the muslin to the sign. Glue a black wood bead to the edge of the lower door's frame. Hang the sign from the bead.

14. Paint a 16mm bead purple. Cut 4 pieces of hemp 4" long and 1 piece 9" long. Thread 2 iridescent beads onto each 4" piece and knot each end. Push a bead down to each knot to form the spider's feet. Gather the 4 pieces and tie the end of the long piece of twine around the middle. Thread the other end through the purple bead and give a little tug so the knot around the legs lodges inside the bead; glue to secure. Trim off the excess hemp. Coil a length of black wire around a pencil. Insert one end of the coiled wire into the top of the spider bead; glue in place. Insert the other end of the wire through the hole in one of the decorative beads on the roof edge; glue in place.

15. Bend the spider legs to form spider knees. Press the legs up onto the spider body and secure with a small amount of glue. Use a toothpick dipped in white acrylic paint to make 2 dots for eyes.

16. Paint four 25mm wood beads black-green. When dry, glue to the underside of the house at the corners for "feet."

17. Add a flying bat to the side of the house by poking a hole in the side of the house and inserting the end of the coiled wire into the hole; secure with a small dot of glue.

Paper Lanterns

by Livia McRee

Hang these festive paper lanterns in front of a window or above your dining table for a luminous effect. A glow stick dangles from the center of each lantern, producing the eerie colored light. Glow sticks are available at party stores, and seasonally at pharmacies. You can also find them in the camping department at discount stores.

Materials

For 3 lanterns, 2 square and 1 triangular
11 sheets of black card stock, 8½" x 11"
11 sheets of vellum, 8½" x 11"
4 rolls of wall mounting foam tape, ½" wide
5½ yards wire-edged silver ribbon, ⅛" wide
3 glow sticks (1 orange, 1 green, 1 blue)
Invisible thread
Ruler
Pencil
Craft knife with several spare blades
Self-healing cutting mat
Bone folder
Tracing paper
Thin cardboard for templates
Double-coated tape

Instructions

1. Using a ruler and pencil, draft a 5⅞" x 10" rectangle on each sheet of black card stock. Cut on the marked lines. Draft a line parallel to and ¾" from each short edge for the top and bottom flaps. Draft a line parallel to and ¼" from the right edge. Cut away the rectangles at the top right and bottom right corners where the lines overlap.

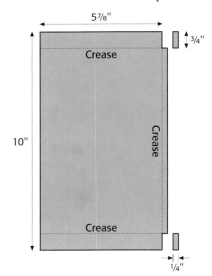

2. Lightly score the paper on the marked lines with a ruler and bone folder (see tip on page 7). Fold the paper on the scored lines. Unfold

the paper; mark a point on the edge of the paper ¼" from each end of each flap. Trim both sides of each flap from the marked point to the inner corner.

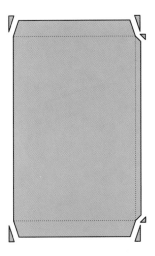

3. Draft a 5½" x 8" rectangle on each sheet of vellum; cut on the marked lines. Set aside.

4. Trace the pumpkin, black cat, and haunted house lantern templates on pages 86–87; glue or tape each tracing securely to a piece of thin cardboard. Place the cardboard on a self-healing cutting mat. Cut out all the white spaces with a craft knife to make 3 templates.

5. Lay the lantern panels flat, wrong side up with the flaps open and the side flaps on the right. Place the lantern templates in the center of the panels, inside the flaps. Trace around the designs; repeat to mark 4 panels for each square lantern and 3 panels for the triangular lantern. Cut on the marked lines.

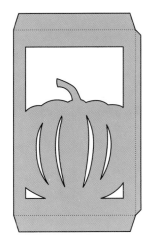

6. Lay out 4 black panels for a rectangular lantern or 3 for a triangular lantern wrong side up. Make 1 lantern at a time. Attach the side flaps to the inside edge of the adjacent panels with double-coated tape. The tape should cover the entire flap. Make sure the crease of the flap is aligned with the edge of the adjacent panel, forming a nice corner. Do not close the lantern yet.

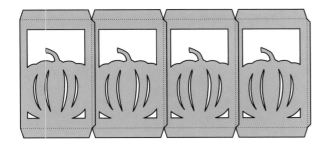

7. Cut two 7" and two 5½" strips of foam mounting tape for each lantern panel. Starting with the second panel, adhere the 5½" foam strips to the top and bottom edges of the panel back and adhere the 7" strips to the side edges of the panel just inside the scored lines. Then lay the vellum rectangle over the foam strips, securing it in place. Fold the top and bottom panel flaps over the vellum, securing with double-coated tape. Continue in the same manner with the third and fourth panel if used.

8. For the first panel, attach the top, bottom, and right foam strips, but do not peel off the backing. Do not fold over the top and bottom flaps yet.

9. Attach a piece of double-coated tape to the back of the entire left edge of the first panel. Bring the last panel over, securing it to the first panel to close the lantern. Attach the last piece of foam tape and secure the vellum in place, then fold over the top and bottom flaps as before.

10. For the square lanterns, cut 2 equal lengths of ribbon, each 30" long or to the desired size. Using double-coated tape, attach each end of 1 ribbon to opposite inside corners, making sure the ribbon runs down the corners at least 2½". Secure the other ribbon to the remaining corners.

    For the triangular lantern, attach the ends of 1 ribbon to 2 corners, then one end of another ribbon to the third corner, letting the remaining end hang loose.

11. To hold the ribbons firmly in place and add strength to the lantern, cut a ¼" x 8½" piece of black card stock from the scraps, for each corner of each lantern (11 total). Lightly score the center of the strip lengthwise with a ruler and bone folder, and attach double-coated tape to the back of the strip. Fold the strip, and press it into a corner of the lantern, covering the ribbon.

12. Gather the ribbons at the center top of the lantern and knot them about 3" down from the center to form a loop for hanging. For the triangular lantern, do the same, trimming off the loose end of the second ribbon, ¼" below the knot. Fold the end over and tuck into the knot.

13. Cut a 28" length of invisible thread. Tie the center of the thread to the knot in the ribbon. Attach a glow stick to the opposite ends of the thread, adjusting the glow stick to the desired height. Trim excess invisible thread.

Candy Corn Candles

by The Wax Barn

Make these unique candy corn candles to light up a dark Halloween night. They are easily made using a cone-shaped candle mold and the simple instructions given below. Instructions are given for both a 5" and 7" candle. Use the two sizes together in a grouping, or make all one size and line them up across a fireplace mantel.

Safety Note: Do not leave burning candles unattended. Place all candles on a fire-safe dish before burning.

Materials

(for one 7" candle or two 5" candles)

9½" cone-shaped mold (Pourette B534B; includes 36" wicking, rod, screw, mold sealer, and instructions)
Mold sealer (puttylike substance)
1 lb. (four 4-oz. bars) paraffin wax
Vybar 103
2 orange Reddig-Glo color chips
1 yellow Reddig-Glo color chip
New sponge (a used sponge may release particles of grit inside your mold)
Dishtowel
Scissors
Masking tape
Skewer
Ruler
3-quart saucepan
Chef's knife
Measuring spoons
3 Candle Magic Boil Bags
Candy or soapmaking thermometer
Timer
Dinner plate
Old frying pan

Instructions

Note: The amounts and measurements for a 7" candle are given first. For a 5" candle, substitute the numbers in parentheses immediately following.

1. Wash the mold in warm, soapy water, and dry thoroughly. Insert the uncut wicking through the small hole on the mold underside, draw it up through the mold, and tie the end securely around the wicking rod. Rest the rod across the rim of the mold, then pull the wicking taut from the other end. Adjust the rod as needed so the wicking is centered within the mold. On the underside, twist the small screw partway into the hole alongside the wicking. Trim the excess wicking, leaving a 1" tail. Wind the tail counterclockwise around the screw shaft, then press mold sealer over the screw to seal the entire area.

2. Wrap a short piece of tape around a long skewer 1⅞" (1⅜") from one end, pressing the tape ends together to make a small flag. Stand the skewer in the mold, flag first, alongside the wicking. Temporarily hold with tape near the top.

3. Fill the saucepan halfway with water, and bring to a boil on the stove. Cut a 4-oz. block of wax into 4 equal pieces. Place 2 oz. (1 oz.) of wax and 1 teaspoon (½ teaspoon) of Vybar in the boil bag; set the bag in boiling water. Adjust the heat to maintain a gentle boil, standing by until the wax is fully melted and appears as clear liquid. Use a thermometer to check the temperature of the wax. When it reaches 180°F to 190°F, it is ready for pouring.

4. Pour the hot liquid wax into the mold, letting it run down the inside wall in a slow, uninterrupted stream until the flag level is reached. If possible, have someone tilt the mold as you begin the pour so the wax does not splatter when it hits the bottom. Lift out the skewer. Let the wax cool about 20 minutes (10 minutes), or until a skin forms on the top. The ideal skin will have a hard outer ring about $\frac{1}{4}$" thick. The interior will give slightly when pressed with a skewer but will not poke through.

> **TIP** ▶ If you pour the second or third layer of wax too soon, before the skin is formed, the new hot wax will melt through the previous layer and the two colors will mix. If you wait too long, a hard line will appear between the colors. You want the colors to blend just a little bit where they meet, for a soft transition.

5. Fit the skewer with a new tape flag $4\frac{1}{4}$" (3") from the bottom end. Stand the skewer on the white wax layer, alongside the wicking, and tape in place temporarily, near the top.

6. Place 10 oz. (5 oz.) wax, $1\frac{1}{2}$ teaspoons ($\frac{1}{2}$ teaspoon) Vybar, and $1\frac{1}{2}$ orange diamond color chips ($\frac{3}{4}$ of an orange diamond color chip) in a new boil bag; cut the whole chips with a knife to obtain the amount needed. Heat and melt the ingredients and check the temperature as in step 3. Pour the liquid orange wax into the mold up to the new flag level, as in step 4. Let cool for about 50 minutes (30 minutes) until the proper skin forms. Meanwhile, pour out the remaining orange wax from the bag onto a dinner plate, making several egg yolk–sized circles. The circles will cool and harden in 3 to 5 minutes and can be easily peeled up for reuse.

7. Attach a new tape flag to the skewer $1\frac{1}{8}$" ($\frac{7}{8}$") from the end. Tape the skewer alongside the wicking. In a new boil bag, place 4 oz. (2 oz.) wax, any leftover white wax from step 4, $\frac{1}{2}$ teaspoon ($\frac{1}{4}$ teaspoon) Vybar, and $\frac{1}{3}$ ($\frac{1}{6}$) of a yellow diamond color chip; melt as before. Spill a small amount of hot yellow wax onto the dinner plate, and let cool. Note the wax's lemon-citron cast. For a warmer yellow, break a piece off one of your orange circles from step 6, and add it to the boil bag; swirl gently until it is melted in. Spill out some of this wax and let cool. The color will appear slightly warmer and more orange. Repeat this testing process, adding orange wax to the yellow wax in small amounts, until you achieve a butter yellow hue. Return all your yellow test chips to the bag and melt them in. When you have achieved the desired butter yellow hue, pour the yellow wax into the mold to the flag level. Remove the skewer.

8. Let the candle cool 4 to 6 hours, or longer, until the metal mold is cool to the touch. To fill the well that develops in the center, melt the remaining wax (you can blend the colors), cool to about 160°F, and pour in slowly to within $\frac{1}{4}$" of the outside edge. Let cool 30 to 60 minutes.

9. Remove the wick rod. Turn the mold upside down on a soft, folded dishtowel. Remove the wick sealer and screw. Tap the mold straight down onto the dishtowel to release the candle. If the candle doesn't release, refrigerate it for a few minutes and try again. Trim the wick at both ends. To even up the bottom surface, stand the candle upright in an old frying pan, set over low heat, and rotate the candle gently over the pan surface for 1 or 2 minutes until even.

Ghost and Skeleton Luminaries

by Livia McRee

Create these spooky luminaries to illuminate your home. Your Halloween guests will be thrilled by their ghostly glow. The designs are etched on the sides of glass flower vases. Simply place a small votive candle inside each one, and use long fireplace matches or a taper candle to light them.

TIP ▶ You can use the templates on page 88 to cut your own stencils from adhesive vinyl following the instructions given below. Or you can order precut vinyl stencils by sending photocopies of the templates to B&B Etching Products; see Sources Guide on page 111. The precut stencils have both a paper backing and a protective top paper. To use the precut stencils, follow the manufacturer's instructions.

Materials

2 rectangular glass vases
Etchall etching creme
Etchall squeegee applicator
Glass cleaner and a lint-free cloth
Access to a photocopier
Adhesive vinyl (Con-Tact paper)
Graphite paper
Tape
Craft knife
Cotton swabs and nail polish remover
Newspaper
Goggles
Plastic gloves

Instructions

1. Clean the vases with glass cleaner. Dry with a lint-free cloth.
2. Photocopy the ghost and skeleton designs on page 88, enlarging or reducing as necessary to fit the sides of your glass vases.
3. Cut out a piece of adhesive vinyl larger than each design. Peel off the paper backing, adhere the vinyl to the vase, and smooth it with the squeegee. Make sure there are no air bubbles or wrinkles.
4. Tape graphite paper to the vinyl. Position the photocopy over both layers and tape securely. Trace over the design lines, then remove the photocopy and graphite paper.
5. Using a craft knife with a new blade, cut the vinyl along the design lines. For clean cuts around curves, try not to lift the blade from the surface but rotate the vase instead. Carefully remove all the surrounding vinyl that is not part of the image. Remove the skeleton eyes and nose, but leave the eyes and mouth for the ghosts.
6. Rub over the vinyl with the squeegee to double-check the adhesion. Look for any smudges of adhesive, especially in the eye or nose areas. To remove smudges, use a cotton swab moistened with nail polish remover, being careful that none gets under the edges of the vinyl.
7. Read through the manufacturer's instructions for applying the etching creme. Protect your work area with newspaper. Put on the goggles and plastic gloves. Turn the vase upside down on a protected surface, and pour out etching creme onto the bottom of the vase. Using the squeegee and working as quickly as possible, pull the creme over each side of the vase in turn, spreading it in an even, smooth layer. Let the creme sit 15 minutes. Use the squeegee to remove the excess creme and return it to the container. Rinse off all the remaining creme under running water, then remove the vinyl. Rinse the vase with water.

Painted Spiderweb
Cake Plate and Ghost Dome

by Carin Heiden Atkins

Make your little ghosts and goblins squeal with delight when you serve up tasty treats from this cake plate and dome. The frosted, glossy, and iridescent ghosts will happily haunt the Halloween festivities in any decor. This easy glass painting project is completed with Pebeo Vitrea 160 glass paint. It's a water cleanup, resin-based paint that is easily made permanent—simply heat-set in your home oven at 325°F for 40 minutes. Once the heat-setting process is complete, your painted glass pieces will be dishwasher-safe.

TIP ▶ You can speed the paint drying process by using a hair dryer.

Materials

Glass cake plate and dome
Pebeo Vitrea 160 Glass Paint
    Cloud (frosted white)
    Veil (gloss white)
    Black
    Saffron Yellow (gloss)
Pebeo Vitrea 160 Transparent Outliner
    Sun Yellow
    Paprika
Pebeo Vitrea 160 Iridescent Medium
Pebeo Vitrea 160 Black Glossy Marker
Glass cleaner and a lint-free cloth
Tracing paper
Pencil
Scissors
Tape
White synthetic brushes: round #6 and #8
    and flat shader #10
Latex makeup sponges
Lazy Susan or cake decorating turntable
    (optional)
Thick-line marking pen

Paint the Ghost Dome

1. Thoroughly clean the glass cake dome with glass cleaner. This step removes grease from the piece and helps the paint adhere better.

2. Make several tracings of the ghost templates on page 90; roughly cut around each tracing. Tape the ghost tracings randomly to the inside of the cake dome as desired. Paint ghosts on the outside of the dome with the cloud white and veil white paints and the #8 round brush, using the tracings visible through the glass as a guide. Shorten some of the ghost tails, if desired. Allow to dry for 10 minutes.

3. Paint over every third ghost with the iridescent medium (I painted over all the glossy white ghosts).

4. Using a latex makeup sponge, apply saffron yellow paint over the the dome pull. Even coverage may require 2 coats. Allow to dry for 10 minutes after each coat.

5. Using the paprika and sun yellow transparent outliners, draw scroll and curlicue patterns over the painted dome pull.

6. Using the sun yellow transparent outliner, add the star pattern freehand below the dome pull, using the photo on page 45 as a guide. Fill in the star with sun yellow; allow to dry. Outline the star with the paprika outliner.

7. Using a #10 flat shader brush and the black paint, create a checkerboard pattern on the lower edge of the dome. Space each square roughly 1 brush width apart, all the way around.

8. Using the tip of your paintbrush handle and black paint, add eyes to the ghost faces. Paint the ring at the base of the dome pull black. Set aside the dome and allow to dry overnight before heat-setting the paints.

Paint the Spiderweb Cake Plate

1. Clean the cake plate with glass cleaner. Trace the spiderweb template on page 89, using the thick-line marking pen. Center the tracing face down on the cake plate and tape in place. Turn the cake plate upside down.
2. Using the Vitrea 160 black marker, trace the spiderweb design on the underside of the cake plate.
3. Sponge the underside of the pedestal with saffron yellow. Allow to dry. Paint the underside of the plate rim saffron yellow.
4. Stand the cake plate upright. On the top surface of the pedestal, paint a scroll and curlicue pattern to match the dome pull.
5. Paint vertical stripes of cloud white on the remaining portion of the cake stand, and cross over them with horizontal wavy stripes of veil white. Accent any rings of the stand with saffron yellow paint. Allow the cake plate to air-dry overnight before heat-setting the paints.

Heat-Set the Paints

Place the painted glassware in a cold oven, then warm the oven to 325°F. Bake the glassware for 40 minutes. When the baking is complete, turn off the oven. Allow the pieces to cool in the oven to avoid cracking or damaging them. Once cooled, your ghostly cake plate and dome are dishwasher-safe and ready to use.

Halloween Treat Bags

by Dave Brethauer

Send your Halloween visitors home with their own special treat bags, filled with delectable goodies. These bags hang from a line tied between two potted driftwood branches and spell out "Halloween." Be sure to weight the bottom of each pot to support the weight of your goody bags. Use a basket to hold extra bags, or display them on the table. Make the lettering for the bags by using a computer and printer, or simply hand-write the letters on the bags with a marking pen.

Materials

2 terra cotta pots, each 6"–7" high and 8"
    across the top
2-oz. bottle celery green acrylic paint
Small, heavy rocks
Floral foam
2 driftwood branches, 2½' to 3' long
Hot glue gun and glue sticks
Moss
Computer and printer
Garamouche font (optional)
9 sheets celery ribbed text weight paper,
    8½" x 11"
Candy or treats to fill bags
3/16" hole punch
3/16" celery green eyelets and eyelet tool
9 circle paper clips
1¼ yards cording
1" flat paintbrush
Metal edge ruler
Pencil
Bone folder
Scissors
Double-coated tape
Hammer

Instructions

1. Paint the terra cotta pots with celery green acrylic paint. Allow to dry.
2. Pack floral foam into the bottom half of the pots. Stand a branch upright in the center of the foam, and secure using hot glue. Fill each pot with rocks to add weight for stability. Lay pieces of moss over the rocks and hot-glue in place.
3. Using a computer and printer, print the letter "H" on a sheet of celery green paper so it falls 3"–5" from the left edge and 3"–4½" from the top edge when "landscape" orientation under Page Setup is used. Use any desired font (I used Garamouche at 120 point). Repeat to print single letters on each remaining sheet to spell out "Halloween."
4. Lay the "H" sheet flat. Score 2 parallel vertical lines (see tip on page 7) 2"–3½" apart, with the "H" midway between them. This section will form the front of the bag (A).
5. Measure out 1" from the scored lines to each side and score 2 more vertical lines to form the bag sides (B and C) as shown.

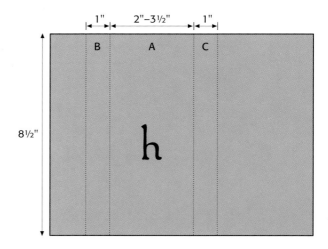

6. Measure the width of the bag front. Measure out this distance from the C side scored line and score a vertical line to form the bag back (D). Score a line 1" from the B side scored line to form a flap. Cut on these last 2 scored lines to trim away the excess paper. Repeat steps 4–6 for each sheet, varying the width of the bag front A.

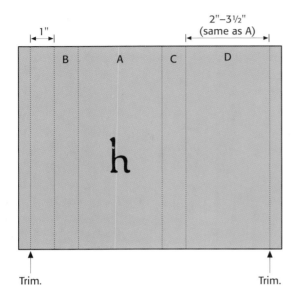

Trim.   Trim.

7. Score a horizontal line 1"–2" from the lower edge. Cut on the vertical scored lines from the lower edge to this horizontal scored line, to form short flaps. Cut away the flap in the lower left corner. Repeat for each sheet.

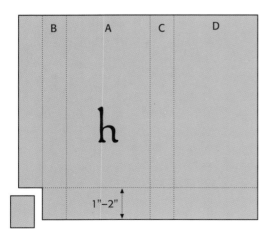

8. Fold along all scored lines. Tape the 1" flap to the wrong side of D, using double-coated tape. To form the bag bottom, fold in the side flaps, then the back and front flaps, trimming if necessary. Secure with double-coated tape. Repeat for each sheet.

9. Fill each paper bag with candy. Press the top edges together and punch a $3/16$" hole through both layers about $1/2$" down from the upper edge. Insert the eyelet through both holes from the front, then turn the bag over. Insert the setting tool into the back of the eyelet and tap with a hammer to set the eyelet.

10. Bend each circle clip into a figure eight. Hook 1 clip through the eyelet in each bag.

11. Tie a length of cording between the driftwood branches, and hang the bags from it. If the hooks slip, tie knots along the cording to keep them evenly spaced.

Ghost and Pumpkin Party Favors

Entertain your ghosts and goblins with these holiday treats. Choose from a ghostly vellum bag of goodies or a pumpkin tin filled with orange and black candies. The favors serve as Halloween tree ornaments when hung from a manzanita branch.

Ghost Treat Bags

by Kathryn Perkins

Materials *(For 1 bag)*

1 sheet vellum with iridescent fleck, $8\frac{1}{2}$" x 11"
Gold metallic thread
$\frac{3}{8}$ yard black organdy ribbon, $\frac{3}{4}$" wide
1 sheet heavy-weight vellum for stencil
Craft knife and self-healing cutting mat
Black pigment ink
Dauber
Sewing machine
Double-coated tape
$\frac{3}{16}$" hole punch
$\frac{3}{16}$" black eyelet and eyelet tool
Hammer
Candy or treats to fill bag

Instructions

1. Trace the ghost face template on page 87 onto the center of heavy-weight vellum. Cut out the ghost face with the craft knife to make a stencil.

2. Align the stencil on the flecked vellum. Use black ink and the dauber to stencil the face onto the flecked vellum. Allow to dry.

3. Roll the paper, generously overlapping the short ends. Flatten the bottom end so the ghost face is centered.

4. Using gold thread, machine-stitch $\frac{1}{4}$" from the lower edge through all the layers. Secure the overlapped sections on the back of the bag with double-coated tape.

5. Continue as on page 50, step 9. Tie ribbon through the eyelet.

Pumpkin Tins

by Kathryn Perkins

Materials *(For 1 tin)*

Orange card stock, $8\frac{1}{2}$" x 11"
Black pigment ink
Glass-topped aluminum tin, $1\frac{1}{2}$" diameter
Green taped floral wire
15" olive organdy ribbon, $\frac{5}{8}$" wide
Pumpkin face rubber stamp from PSX, B035
Scissors
Burnisher
Pencil
Darning needle
Halloween candy

Instructions

1. Set the tin on the orange card stock and trace around it with a pencil. Cut just outside the marked line.

2. Stamp the pumpkin face in the center of the orange circle with black pigment ink; allow to dry. Insert the pumpkin face into the glass lid from the underside. Use a burnisher to press the paper snugly into the lid.

3. Fill the tin with orange and black Halloween candy. Replace the lid.

4. Cut a 24" length of floral wire. Wrap once around the tin, and twist to secure. Wind the ends around a pencil and darning needle to make spirals of varying widths. Wrap the organdy ribbon around the tin, over the wire, and tie the ends in a bow.

Appliquéd Pumpkin Table Runner and Napkins

by Linda Johnson

C reate this appliquéd table runner to adorn your dining table or buffet. The design makes it suitable for use throughout autumn. For a matched look, create a set of coordinating appliquéd napkins with frayed edges.

Materials

42"-wide cotton fabrics:

    1⅜ yards for the center background and backing, plus ½ yard per 2 napkins

    ¼ yard total of brown scraps (2 pieces must be 1" x 30½")

    ⅔ yard for the outer border and binding

    ¼ yard for the pumpkin appliqués

    ¼ yard total of green scraps for the leaf appliqués

    Yellow scraps for the star and moon appliqués

Green #5 perle cotton for the vines on the table runner

20" x 50" rectangle of batting

Green floss for the vines on the napkins

Sewing machine

Iron and ironing board

General sewing tools

Hand quilting needle

Embroidery needle

Thread to match fabrics

Safety pins

Chalk pencil

Cut the Fabrics

Note: Patterns and templates can be found on pages 91–94.

For the table runner, cut the following pieces:

From the background/backing fabric, cut:

    1 rectangle, 10" x 30½", for the table runner front

    1 rectangle, 20" x 50", for the table runner back

From the brown fabric scraps, cut:

    2 strips, each 1" x 30½", for the narrow inner side borders

    18 triangles using pattern A

From the outer border/binding fabric, cut:

    4 end border pieces using pattern B

    2 side border pieces using pattern C (lengthen pattern C so it measures 30" from dot to dot)

    3 strips, each 2½" x 44", for the binding

From the pumpkin appliqué fabric, cut:

    2 large pumpkins (use both patterns)

From the green fabric scraps, cut:

    12 leaves

    2 different pumpkin stems

From the yellow fabric scraps, cut:

    1 moon

    2 stars

For each napkin, cut the following pieces:

From the napkin fabric, cut:

    1 square, 18" x 18"

From the pumpkin appliqué fabric, cut:

    1 small pumpkin

From the green fabric scraps, cut:

    1 small pumpkin stem

From the yellow fabric scraps, cut:

    1 small moon or 1 small star

Make the Table Runner Top

Note: Join all pieces with a ¼" seam allowance.

1. Stitch the narrow brown inner border pieces to the long edges of the center background piece. Press seam allowances toward the inner border.

2. Stitch 2 different brown triangles together along the long edges. Repeat to make 6 triangle squares.

Make 6.

3. Stitch 3 brown triangle squares to 3 brown triangles to make a pieced triangle as shown for the point of the table runner. Repeat to make a second large pieced triangle.

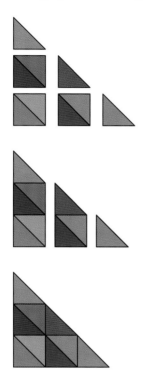

4. Stitch 1 large pieced triangle to each short edge of the center background piece.

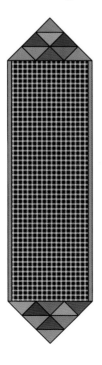

5. Stitch 1 outer border piece C to each long edge of the center background piece, starting and stopping at the dots.

6. At one end of the runner, sew 1 end border piece B to each edge of the large pieced triangle; stitch from dot to dot.

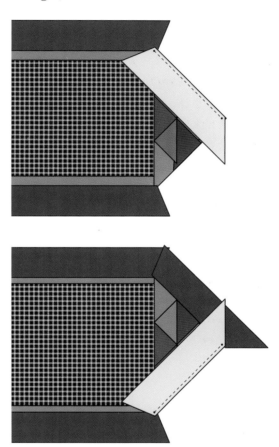

7. Stitch the B pieces together from the dot to the outer edge to form the runner point.

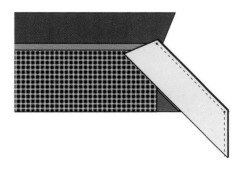

8. Stitch each B piece to the adjacent C piece in the same way.

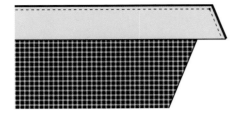

9. Repeat at the other end of the runner.
10. Pin the appliqué pieces to the table runner top, using the Appliqué Placement Guide on page 57 as a guide.
11. Turn under the raw edge of each appliqué piece for 1"–2", creasing with your finger. Slipstitch the piece in place, taking stitches about ⅛" apart. Continue to turn under the raw edges of the appliqué with your needle 1"–2" ahead of your stitching. Clip inside corners and trim excess fabric across outside corners of the appliqué to reduce bulk. Make stitches closer together around curves and points as necessary. Appliqué pieces closest to the background first and pieces that overlap last.
12. Using a chalk pencil, draw in vine stems on the table runner, using the Appliqué Placement Guide on page 57 as a guide. Using green #5 perle cotton, backstitch the vine stems (see "Embroider the Blocks" on page 28). Start at the top of the pumpkin and make 3 rows of stitching close together, tapering to 1 row at the ends for the curls. Be careful not to pull the stitches too tight.

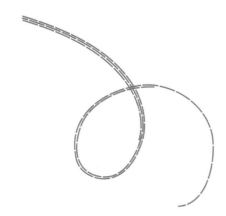

Assemble the Table Runner

1. Place the backing fabric right side down and layer with batting. Place the table runner top right side up on the batting. Baste the layers together with safety pins, spacing them about 4" apart.
2. Hand-quilt on the dashed lines as indicated on the appliqué patterns. Quilt additional lines of stitching as desired. Trim the batting and backing even with the edges of the table runner top.
3. Join the binding strips in diagonal seams; trim the seam allowances to ¼" (see page 29, step 4, for detail)
4. Press the binding in half lengthwise, wrong side in. Position the raw edges of the binding even with the raw edges of the table runner top. Stitch the binding ¼" from the raw edges, leaving at least 3" unstitched at the beginning. Stop stitching ¼" from the corner; backstitch and remove the table runner from the machine.
5. Fold the binding up at the corner, then fold it down, keeping the raw edge even with the adjacent side of the table runner.

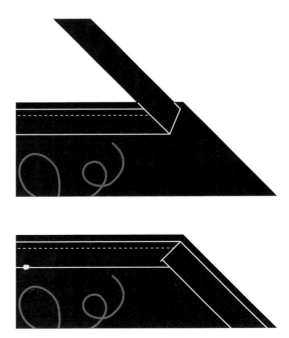

6. Begin stitching off the edge of the fabric at the corner and continue until you are ¼" from the next corner; backstitch and remove the runner from the machine. Repeat step 5. Continue in the same manner around the remainder of the table runner. When you return to the starting point, turn under and overlap the ends, trimming off any excess.

7. Fold the binding onto the runner back, mitering the corners. Pin in place, just covering the stitching line. Hand stitch in place (see page 66, step 10, for detail).

Make the Napkins

1. Fray all 4 edges of each napkin square by removing threads to make a ½" fringe. Set the machine for a narrow zigzag stitch. Stitch just to the left of the fringe all around.

2. Appliqué the pumpkin stem in place, then the pumpkin, following step 11 of "Make the Table Runner Top" on page 56. Appliqué the moon or star in place. Backstitch a green stem on the pumpkin, using embroidery floss.

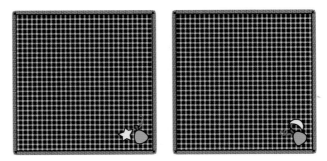

Appliqué Placement Guide
Napkins

Appliqué Placement Guide
Table Runner

Photo Transfer Halloween Place Mats and Napkins

by Sandy Bonsib

Customize a set of linen place mats and napkins with transfers of vintage Halloween images. These are so simple to make, you can create an entire set in an afternoon with no sewing at all. Wash your completed place mats and napkins in cool or warm water as needed (do not use bleach or fabric softener), and lay them flat to dry. Iron at a medium to hot setting. Since transfer papers may vary, follow the manufacturer's instructions for ironing over the transfers.

Materials

Linen place mats and napkins
Copyright-free Halloween images
Access to a color photocopy machine
Photo transfer paper
Scissors
Iron

Instructions

1. Place your Halloween image face down on the glass of a color copy machine. Set the color copier to a "mirror image" setting. This ensures that the image is facing the right way on your place mats and napkins. Adjust the settings to reduce or enlarge the image as desired. Copy the image onto the shiny side of the photo transfer paper, feeding it 1 page at a time into the bypass tray of the copier.

2. Carefully cut each image from the transfer paper, using scissors or a craft knife and self-healing cutting mat. You can cut exactly on the outline of the image or leave a thin ⅛" edge, which is what I did. My edge did not show on the light-colored linen.

3. To transfer your images, use an iron set on the hottest temperature with no steam. Remove any lint from the place mats and napkins before pressing. Position each image face down in the desired position on the right side of the desired linen. On the place mats, you can center the image or place it off to one side. On the napkins, place it diagonally in the corner. Press the images for 25–30 seconds using maximum pressure. Press on a firm, smooth, flat surface such as a tabletop. Position smaller images directly under the soleplate. For larger images, move the iron to press the entire image, holding it down in each position for the required amount of time. See Tip below.

4. Peel off the photo transfer paper immediately after pressing, while it is still hot. If you have trouble peeling off the paper, simply reheat it for a few seconds before trying again. If needed, slightly reheat the fabric to smooth out any distortions.

TIP ▶ Make extra photocopies of the images and practice pressing them on a similar fabric before pressing your actual linens. Make sure your pressing surface is firm, flat, and smooth. Avoid using wood because the grain line may show through. Also, do not use your padded ironing board cover. You may want to lower your pressing surface so you can place as much of your weight over the iron as possible. Depending on your fabric, you may also need to adjust the pressing time.

Patches: The Pumpkin Patch Protector

by Jaynette Huff

Make this scarecrow wall hanging easily by using the paper-piecing technique. In addition to the paper piecing, this scarecrow has a floppy collar, buttons on his shirt, and a twine belt for dimensional interest. Pumpkin-colored buttons give depth to the pumpkin patch. The finished quilt measures 24" x 36" and is the perfect size for a door. Hang this design in your kitchen or foyer during the entire autumn season.

Materials

42"-wide cotton fabrics:
> ⅓ yard for scarecrow background/sky
> ¼ yard for scarecrow flesh, 3-D collar, pieced inner border #2, and corner pumpkin blocks
> ⅓ yard for land and pieced inner border #2
> ⅛ yard for scarecrow pants and pieced inner border #2
> ⅛ yard for orange pumpkin #1 and pieced inner border #2
> ¼ yard for inner borders #1 and #3
> ½ yard for outer border and binding
> 1 yard for backing and rod pocket

Assorted cotton fabric scraps:
> 8" x 11" orange piece for pumpkin #2
> 6" x 9" piece for hat
> 6" x 9" deep dark piece for hat lining, hatband, and belt
> 6" x 9" piece for wood
> 6" x 6" piece for jacket cuffs
> 9" x 11" piece for jacket
> 6" x 6" piece for shirt
> 6" x 6" piece for pant cuffs
> 7" x 9" black piece for crows

> 6" x 6" piece for pumpkin stems
> Patches for jacket and pants

27" x 40" rectangle of batting

Black embroidery floss for the scarecrow face and buttonhole stitching around "patches" and "crows"

2 buttons for shirt

Twine for belt bow

10–15 orange buttons for pumpkins in the field

Neutral thread

Paper for collar pattern

Freezer paper

Pencil

Scissors

Colored marker

Iron and ironing board

Sewing machine

General sewing tools

Tweezers

Rotary cutter, guide, and self-healing mat

Safety pins (size 0 or 1)

Cut the Fabrics

Cut the following pieces, then use the remaining fabrics in the scarecrow and corner blocks.

From each fabric for inner border #2, cut:
> 1 strip, 1½" x 42" (4 strips total)

From fabric for inner borders #1 and #3, cut:
> 6 strips, each 1" x 42" (each border requires 3 strips)

From the outer border/binding fabric, cut:
> 3 strips, each 3½" x 42", for the outer borders
> 3 strips, each 2" x 42", for the binding

Sewing Order (Quilt Center)

Refer to "Piece the Scarecrow Block" on this page for sewing instructions.

Part A: 1–5
Part B: 1–3
> Join A to B (AB)

Part C: 1–2
Part D: 1–3
> Join C to D (CD)

Part E: 1–2
> Join CD to E (CDE)
> Join CDE to AB (ABCDE)

Part F: 1–10
Part G: 1–3
> Join F to G (FG)

Part H: 1–10
> Join FG to H (FGH)

Insert 3-D collar between ABCDE and FGH, and join (ABCDEFGH). To do this, lay the collar on top of the dotted placement line on the foundation. When sewing, be sure to catch the top raw edge of the collar in the seam.

Part I: 1–4
Part J: 1–3
> Join I to J (IJ)

Part K: 1–5
> Join IJ TO K (IJK)
> Join ABCDEFGH to IJK (ABCDEFGHIJK)

Part L: 1–3
Part M: 1–4
> Join L to M (LM)

Part N: 1–10
> Join LM to N (LMN)

Part O: 1–6
Part P: 1–9
> Join O to P (OP)

Part Q: 1–4
> Join OP to Q (OPQ)

Part R: 1–9
> Join OPQ to R (OPQR)
> Join LMN to OPQR (LMNOPQR)

Part S: 1–3
Part T: 1–10
> Join S to T (ST)
> Join LMNOPQR to ST (LMNOPQRST)

> Join ABCDEFGHIJK to LMNOPQRST
> (ABCDEFGHIJKLMNOPQRST)

Sewing Order (Pumpkin Corner Blocks)

Refer to "Piece the Scarecrow Block" below for sewing instructions.

Part A: 1–4
Part B: 1–8
Join A to B (AB)

Piece the Scarecrow Block

1. Using the fabric key below, make a swatch chart for easier fabric control and identification.

Fabric Key (Quilt Center)

BK — Background/Sky
H — Hat
DD — Deep Dark
F — Flesh
W — Wood
JC — Jacket Cuff
J — Jacket
S — Shirt
P — Pants
PC — Pants Cuff
L — Land
ST — Stem of Pumpkin
O1 — Orange Pumpkin #1
O2 — Orange Pumpkin #2

Fabric Key (Pumpkin Corner Blocks)

F — Flesh
O1 or O2 — Orange Pumpkin #1 or Orange Pumpkin #2 (make two blocks using #1 and two blocks using #2)
ST — Stem of Pumpkin

2. Trace or photocopy the collar pattern on page 104. Cut 2 collar pieces from collar fabric F. Pin the collar pieces right sides together; stitch ¼" from the raw edges, leaving the straight upper edge unstitched. Trim the seam allowances and clip all corners. Turn right side out; press. Set the collar aside.

3. Trace the foundation patterns for the scarecrow block on pages 95–104 onto the matte side of the freezer paper. As you trace, join Part A-1 to Part A-2 to make a single pattern, then join Part B-1 to Part B-2 and Part K-1 to Part K-2, matching the parts at the X's. Be sure to carefully and accurately transfer the sewing order numbers (A1, A2, A3, etc.), as well as the fabric designations within the small circles (BK, W, etc.). Trim off excess freezer paper around the outer edges. Notice that the pattern is the mirror image of the finished design.

4. On the pattern, dashed lines separate parts and solid lines separate pattern pieces within the parts. Do not cut on the solid lines; they are your sewing lines.

5. Sew a complete block of "Patches, the Pumpkin Patch Protector" for the quilt center. Refer to the sewing order on page 62, using it as a step-by-step road map of the precise order in which to piece or sew the block. Begin with Part A. Locate A1 and its corresponding fabric. From the fabric, roughly cut out a piece large enough to cover that area completely with at least a ¼" seam allowance all around. Place the fabric right side up on the shiny side of the freezer paper over the area marked A1; iron in place.

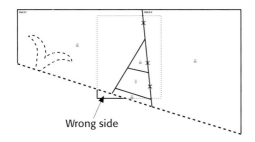
Wrong side

6. Consult your swatch chart and cut a piece of fabric larger all around than A2. Locate the solid line (the sewing line between A1 and A2). Place the fabric piece for A2 over A1, right sides together, with 1 edge at least ¼" beyond the sewing line. Turn the entire sandwich over and view by holding up to the light. Most of piece 2 should be behind piece 1; check the position and adjust, if necessary. On the matte side of the foundation pattern, stitch on the line between A1 and A2, using 15 to 20 stitches per inch.

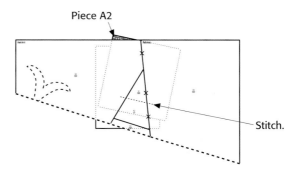
Piece A2

Stitch.

7. Crease the foundation pattern along the sewing line. Trim the excess fabric to a scant ¼" along the sewing line.

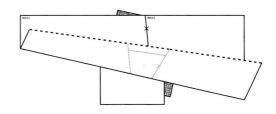

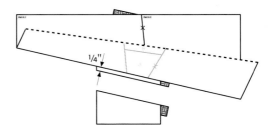
¼"

8. Fold the foundation paper back down. Flip down the newly attached fabric piece; iron in place, pressing on the matte side first, then on the fabric side. Trim excess fabric, leaving plenty around all edges for seam allowances.

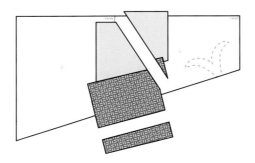

9. Continue stitching together all pieces in Part A in the same manner. When finished, with you rotary cutter trim the fabric exactly $\frac{1}{4}$" around the outer edges of Part A.

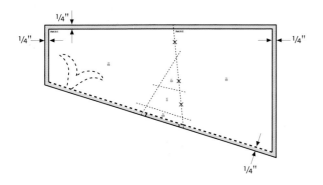

10. Follow the sewing order on page 62 for the next step, joining Part B as for Part A. Then join Parts A and B (AB) as indicated in the sewing order. Pin Part A to Part B, using the quilt assembly diagram on page 97 as a guide. Stitch $\frac{1}{4}$" from the raw edges. Check the piece for accurate matching. Press the seam allowances in the direction of least resistance. Press seam allowances open, if necessary, to reduce bulk. Continue to paper-piece parts, then join parts as for AB until all parts A–T are completely joined.

11. Staystitch $\frac{1}{8}$" from the outer edges of the quilt top. Remove the freezer paper, using tweezers to remove paper from tiny corners or crevices.

Add the Borders

1. Measure the quilt top vertically through the center. From the fabric strips for inner border #1, cut 2 pieces to this length (approximately $26\frac{1}{2}$"). Stitch the pieces to the side edges of the quilt. Press the seam allowances toward the inner border.

2. Measure the quilt top horizontally through the center. From the remaining fabric strip for inner border #1, cut 2 pieces to this length (approximately 16"). Stitch the pieces to the top and bottom of the quilt. Press the seam allowances toward the inner border.

3. Arrange the 4 strips for border #2 in a pleasing order; join along the lengthwise edges. Press the seam allowances to 1 side.

4. Crosscut the unit into $1\frac{1}{2}$"-wide segments, using the rotary cutter. You will need approximately 23 segments for inner border #2.

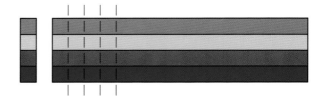

5. Stitch 7 segments together, end to end, for each side border. Stitch 4 segments together, end to end, for the top border. Repeat for the bottom border.

6. Pin a side inner border #2 piece to the left side of the quilt, allowing 1 square of the border to extend beyond the top edge; stitch to within 3" of the top edge. Stitch the bottom

inner border #2 piece to the lower edge, maintaining the color sequence. Stitch a side inner border #2 piece to the right edge of the quilt. Stitch the top inner border #2 piece to the top of the quilt. Finish stitching the inner border on the left side. Press the seam allowances toward inner border #2.

7. Measure the quilt top vertically through the center. From the fabric strips for inner border #3, cut 2 pieces to this length (approximately 29"); stitch the pieces to the side edges of the quilt. Press the seam allowances toward inner border #2.

8. Measure the quilt top horizontally through the center. From the remaining fabric strips for inner border #3, cut 2 pieces to this length (approximately 18"). Stitch the pieces to the top and bottom edges of the quilt. Press the seams toward border #2.

9. Paper-piece 4 pumpkin corner blocks, using the pattern on page 104 and following the Fabric Key and Sewing Order on page 60.

10. Measure the quilt top vertically through the center. From the outer border strips, cut 2 pieces to this length for the side outer borders. Measure the quilt top horizontally through the center. From the outer border strips, cut 2 pieces to this length for the top and bottom outer borders.

11. Stitch a corner block to each end of the top and bottom outer border strips, making sure the pumpkins are right side up.

Top and Bottom Outer Borders
with Corner Pumpkin blocks
Make 2.

12. Stitch the side outer border strips to the side edges of the quilt. Press the seam allowances toward inner border #3. Stitch the top and bottom outer border strips to the quilt. Press the seam allowances toward inner border #3.

Quilt Plan

Assemble the Wall Hanging

1. Cut 4 patches from scraps of fabric, using the patterns on page 104. Appliqué the patches on the scarecrow's jacket and pants, using a buttonhole stitch and black embroidery floss.

Buttonhole Stitch

2. Cut out 7 black crows, using the pattern on page 104. Appliqué the crows to the quilt, using a buttonhole stitch.

3. Embroider the details of the scarecrow face, using a stem stitch. Satin-stitch the nose.

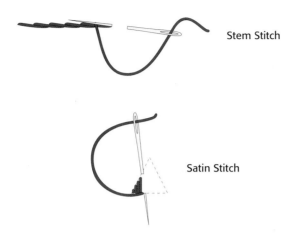

Stem Stitch

Satin Stitch

4. Place the backing fabric right side down and layer with batting. Place the quilt top right side up on the batting. Baste the layers together with safety pins spaced 4" apart.

5. Machine-quilt areas of the scarecrow, stitching in the ditch between pieces. Stitch in the ditch between the center block and inner border #1 and also between inner border #3 and the outer border. Trim the edges of the backing and batting even with the quilt top.

6. Measure the width of the quilt and subtract 2". Cut a 6"-wide fabric strip to this length. Fold in each short end ¼"; repeat, then stitch down along the first fold. Fold the strip in half lengthwise, wrong side in. Center the strip on the back top edge of the quilt, matching raw edges; pin in place.

7. Join the binding strips by stitching a diagonal seam; trim the seam allowances to ¼" (see page 29, step 4, for detail). Press the binding in half lengthwise, wrong side in. Position the raw edges of the binding even with the raw edges of the quilt top along the bottom edge. Stitch the binding to the quilt top ¼" from the raw edges, leaving at least 3" unstitched at the beginning. Stop stitching ¼" from the corner; backstitch and remove the quilt from the machine.

8. Fold the binding up at the corner, making a 45-degree angle. Then fold the binding straight down, aligning the fold with the edge of the quilt. The raw edges of the binding are now even with the next side.

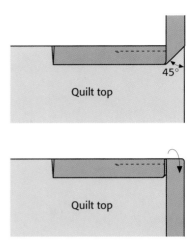

45°

Quilt top

Quilt top

9. Begin stitching off the edge of the fabric at the corner and continue until you are ¼" from the next corner; backstitch and remove the quilt from the machine. Repeat step 8. Continue in the same manner around the quilt. When you return to the starting point, turn under and overlap the ends, trimming any excess.

10. Fold the binding to the back of the quilt; pin in place, just covering the stitching line. Hand stitch the binding in place. Miter the corners; hand stitch in place. Slipstitch the folded edge of the rod pocket to the back of the quilt.

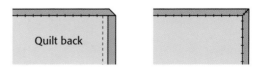

Quilt back

11. Sew buttons on the scarecrow's shirt. Sew a piece of twine to the pants waistband. Tie the twine in a bow and knot the ends. Sew 10–15 orange buttons in the field to suggest additional pumpkins.

Pumpkin Heads

by Jenni Paige

Add some amusement to your kitchen or family room with a grouping of comical pumpkins. These interesting characters with poseable arms can sit neatly on a table or perch on a shelf where their long floppy legs can dangle over the edge. Textural interest is created on the bodies by leaving raw fabric edges exposed on the outer shells of the pumpkins. The fabric shells are washed before being stuffed, to maximize the frayed texture.

Materials

42"-wide cotton fabrics:

$\frac{1}{2}$ yard for outer pumpkin shell (large pumpkin)

$\frac{1}{2}$ yard for inner pumpkin shell (large pumpkin)

$\frac{3}{8}$ yard outer pumpkin shell (medium pumpkin)

$\frac{3}{8}$ yard inner pumpkin shell (medium pumpkin)

$\frac{1}{4}$ yard outer pumpkin shell (small pumpkin)

$\frac{1}{4}$ yard inner pumpkin shell (small pumpkin)

$\frac{1}{8}$ yard for tendril (each pumpkin)

$\frac{1}{8}$ yard for arms (each pumpkin)

$\frac{1}{8}$ yard for legs and stem (each pumpkin)

Scraps of fabric for shoes, hands, and facial features

Scraps of felted wool or acrylic felt for eyelids

Buttons for eyes (slightly smaller than eyelid pattern, page 108)

Polyester fiberfill

7 chenille stems

Thread to match fabrics

Washing machine and dryer

Iron and ironing board

Permanent marking pen

Freezer paper

Sewing machine

General sewing tools

Fray preventer

Safety pins

Wooden spoon

Instructions

1. Prewash all fabrics. Iron them smooth.
2. Use the permanent pen to trace the patterns on pages 108–110 onto the matte side of freezer paper. For 1 pumpkin, mark 3 outer pumpkin shells, 3 inner pumpkin shells, 1 nose, 2 feet, 2 hands, 1 mouth, 1 stem, and 2 eyelids. Cut out the 15 paper templates.
3. Fold the outer pumpkin shell fabric in half, right side in. Place the outer pumpkin shell template on the fabric, matte side up, and with a hot, dry iron, quickly press in place. The shiny side will adhere to the fabric. Pin to prevent shifting, then cut along the pattern outline through both layers to make 2 outer pumpkin shell pieces. Remove and discard the freezer paper template. Repeat to cut 6 pieces total. Cut 6 inner pumpkin shells in the same manner.
4. Center each inner pumpkin shell on an outer shell, right sides up, and pin. Stitch $\frac{1}{4}$" in from the inner shell edge through both layers all around.
5. Pin 2 layered shell pieces right sides together. Stitch together along 1 edge, using a $\frac{1}{4}$" seam allowance; be careful not to catch the inner shell in the seam. Stitch a third shell piece to this unit in the same manner. Set this pumpkin half aside. Repeat to make a second pumpkin half.
6. Use the nose template to cut 1 nose from scrap fabric. Pin the nose to the middle section of one of the pumpkin halves, slightly above the midpoint. Stitch $\frac{1}{8}$" from the raw edges of the nose.
7. Place the 2 pumpkin halves right sides together and pin all around. Fold in half to locate the midpoint of each pinned side seam, then mark $1\frac{1}{4}$" openings at these two spots for the arms. Mark a $2\frac{1}{2}$" opening at the top for the stem and tendril. Mark a 6" opening at the bottom for the legs. Stitch completely around the pumpkin, leaving openings as marked; backstitch as you start and stop the stitching. Apply fray preventer around all openings; turn the pumpkin right side out. Set aside.
8. Fold the fabric for the feet *wrong* side in. Fuse the 2 foot patterns to it, as for the pumpkin shells, allowing at least $\frac{1}{2}$" between the pieces for seam allowances. Set the machine to 15 to 20 stitches to the inch. Stitch around the outer edges of the

patterns, leaving openings at the ankles, as indicated on the patterns. Trim excess fabric ¼" from the stitching on the large pumpkin foot and ⅛" from the stitching on the medium and small pumpkin feet. Remove the paper templates. Prepare 2 hands and 1 mouth in the same manner, using the appropriate fabrics. Do not leave an opening for the mouth.

9. Use safety pins to attach the hands, feet, and mouth to your pumpkin. Turn wrong side out. Throw it all into the washing machine with a towel or small load of laundry. Machine-wash and tumble-dry.

10. Remove the pumpkin from the dryer. Turn it right side out and give it a good shake to help smooth any wrinkles. Trim off any large thread tangles. Unpin the pieces.

11. Fold the stem fabric *right* side in. Fuse and sew using the stem pattern, as in step 8. Trim the seam allowance, and turn right side out. Stuff lightly with polyester fiberfill, stopping ¾" from the open end.

12. From the tendril fabric, cut a 1½" x 15" strip. Fold the strip in half lengthwise, right side in. Stitch along the long raw edge and across a short end, making a ¼" seam. Turn right side out. Insert a chenille stem. Set aside.

13. From the arm fabric, cut 1 strip, 2½" x 15" for the large pumpkin, or 2" x 12½" for the medium pumpkin, or 1½" x 6" for the small pumpkin. Fold the strip in half lengthwise, right side in, and stitch the long edges together; cut in half. Insert 3 chenille stems into each arm (the fabric should be loose). Stuff each hand with polyester fiberfill. Insert an arm ½" into each hand opening; stitch closed through all layers, going carefully over the chenille stems. From the leg fabric, cut 1 strip 2½" x 40½" for the large pumpkin, or 2" x 23" for the medium pumpkin, or 1½" x 11" for the small pumpkin. Make the legs and attach the feet in the same way as for the arms, but omit the chenille stems.

14. Turn the pumpkin wrong side out. Pin the stem, tendril, arms, and legs in place. (Remember this is the wrong side of your pumpkin, so everything goes inside.) Be careful to pull the chenille stems in the arms and tendril out far enough so they will catch securely in the seam allowances. Stitch everything securely in place, leaving the bottom open for turning.

15. Carefully turn the pumpkin right side out; don't tug too hard on the arms. Stuff your pumpkin with small pieces of polyester fiberfill, using a wooden spoon to pack it in firmly. Slipstitch the opening closed.

16. Cut a small slit in the back of the mouth; stuff firmly with polyester fiberfill. Hand stitch the opening closed. Machine-stitch across the center of the mouth to divide the lips. Hand stitch the mouth to the pumpkin.

17. Cut 2 eyelids from felt, using the templates. Top each eyelid with a button and stitch in place on the pumpkin head using embroidery floss. Curl the tendril around a pencil. Curl or shape arms in a zigzag fashion.

Halloween Hooked Rugs

Designed by Little Quilts • Hooked by Randy Hamil

This collection of hooked rugs can be displayed on a wall, individually or arranged in a group. Each finished rug measures 9" x 12". These rugs are hooked with wool fabrics. You can build a collection of wool for hooking by searching for wool shirts, skirts, slacks, and other garments at thrift shops. Hand-dyed wool is available through mail-order companies. The black wool used in these projects was taken from a variety of pieces, and the color that results is often referred to as "antique black." This adds depth to the hooking.

Materials

For all rugs:
1½ yard 60"-wide or 45"-wide linen or angus burlap foundation fabric
Black wool yarn for binding
Rug cutting machine; rotary cutter, cutting mat, and ruler; or long scissors, for cutting wool into strips
Masking tape
½ yard nylon net for transferring the designs
Permanent black marking pen
Pins
Rug hooking frame or quilt hoop
Primitive rug hook
Small scissors
Damp press cloth
Iron
Fray preventer
Tapestry needle

Scaredy-Cat

¼ yard "dirty" gold wool for background
3" x 12" orange plaid wool for border strip and star outline
3" x 12" orange wool for star
3" x 12" purple wool for star and cat's nose
½" x 12" purple plaid wool for star outline
½" x 12" dark gray wool for outline of cat's face
⅛ yard black wool for cat and border strips
½" x 12" oatmeal tweed wool for whiskers
Small scrap green or gold wool for cat's eyes

Happy Jack

3" x 18" orange plaid wool for pumpkin outline
9" x 18" orange wool for pumpkin
6" x 18" gold plaid wool for border
¼ yard black wool for background
3" x 12" green plaid wool for leaf outlines
3" x 12" green wool for leaves
3" x 12" tweed wool for stem outline
3" x 12" camel wool for stem
3" x 12" gold plaid wool for star outlines
3" x 12" gold wool for stars
3" x 12" white wool for teeth

"Boo"

¼ yard purple wool for background
9" x 12" black wool for border
12" x 12" plaid wool for border and letter outlines
3" x 12" tweed wool for star outlines
3" x 12" gold wool for star
6" x 12" oatmeal tweed wool for letters

Instructions

1. Wash and dry all the wool fabric. Cut the wool fabric into long ¼"-wide strips; cut the strips slightly narrower for smaller areas of the designs.

> **TIP** ▶ Cut your wool strips using a rug cutting machine or a rotary cutter and cutting mat. To cut strips with a pair of scissors, snip the wool ½" wide, tear the strip, and then cut the strip in half lengthwise.

2. Cut a rectangle approximately 21" x 24" from the foundation fabric for each design. Cover the edges with masking tape to prevent them from fraying.

3. Trace the designs on pages 105–107 onto the nylon net using the permanent black marking pen. Center each transferred design on a piece of foundation fabric, lining up straight lines such as borders with the weave whenever possible. Pin the net to the foundation. Use the same marker to draw over the design carefully. The marker will go through the holes, transferring the design. Fill in any unconnected areas.

4. Place the marked burlap in a quilt hoop or on a rug hooking frame. Hold a wool strip underneath the design with one hand. On the marked side, with your free hand, insert the rug hook just inside an outline of the design and pull the end of the strip up through a hole about ½". Beginning and ending strips are pulled to the top and left longer; they are trimmed even with the loops later. Following the design, reinsert the hook into the foundation fabric and pull the wool strip up through the fabric on the hook; release the loop when it is pulled ¼" through to the right side of the fabric. Repeat, spacing

loops 2 threads apart in the foundation fabric. Keep the loop height consistent.

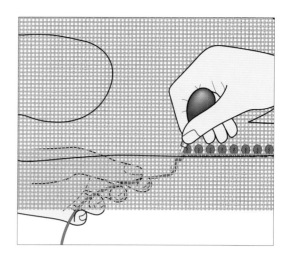

5. Outline each section of the design, hooking just inside the marked line, then fill in. Hook single design lines on the marking. Hook a line around the outer edge of the background, then fill in the background as desired. Hook borders in straight lines all the way around. Trim all beginning and ending strips even with the loops.

6. Cover the rug with a damp cloth; steam and press to flatten. Allow to dry flat. Trim excess burlap ¼" from the hooked edge. Spread a thin layer of fray preventer over the raw edges to prevent raveling; allow to dry.

7. Using the black wool yarn, overcast the edges, binding the rug. Steam-press again and dry flat.

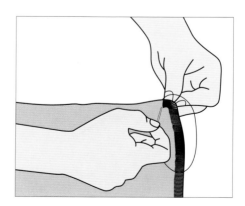

Patterns

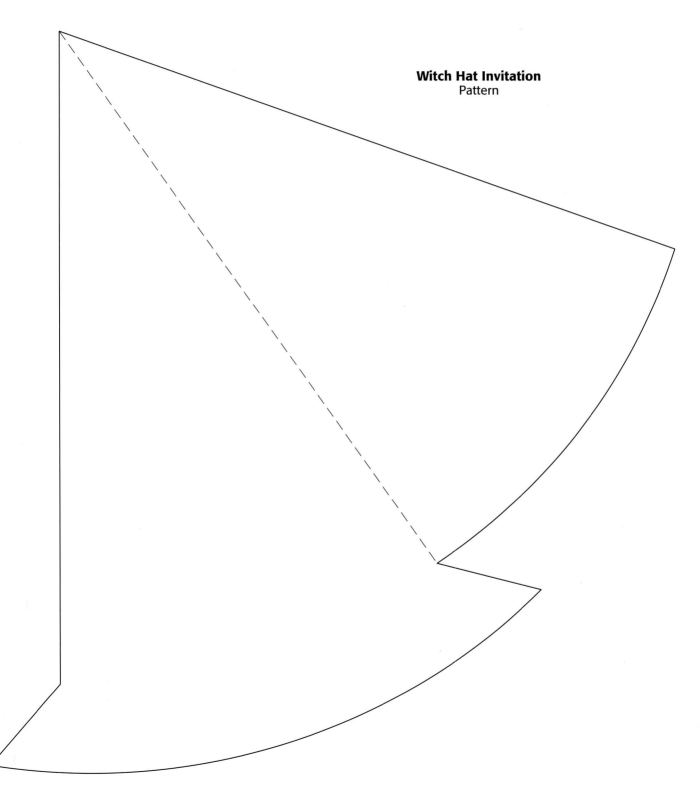

Witch Hat Invitation
Pattern

Casing foldline

Stitching
placement line

Stitching
placement lines

Halloween Cat Banner
Pattern

Enlarge 250%.

TOP

Carved Witch Pumpkin
Pattern

Painted Floor Cloth
Pattern

Enlarge 400%.

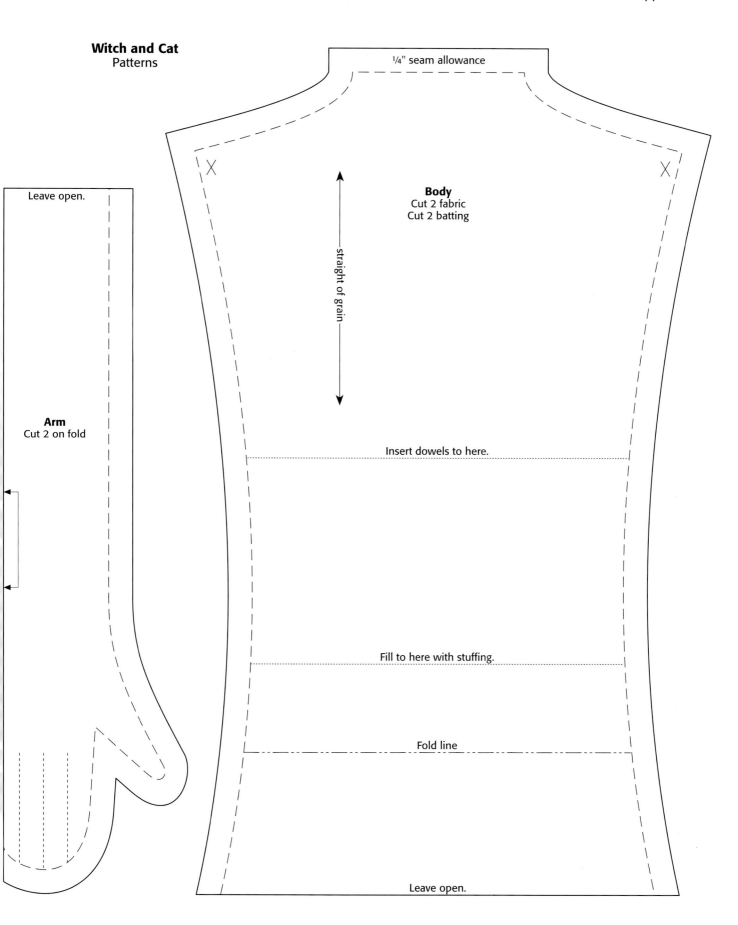

Witch and Cat
Patterns

Leave open.

Arm
Cut 2 on fold

Body
Cut 2 fabric
Cut 2 batting

¼" seam allowance

straight of grain

Insert dowels to here.

Fill to here with stuffing.

Fold line

Leave open.

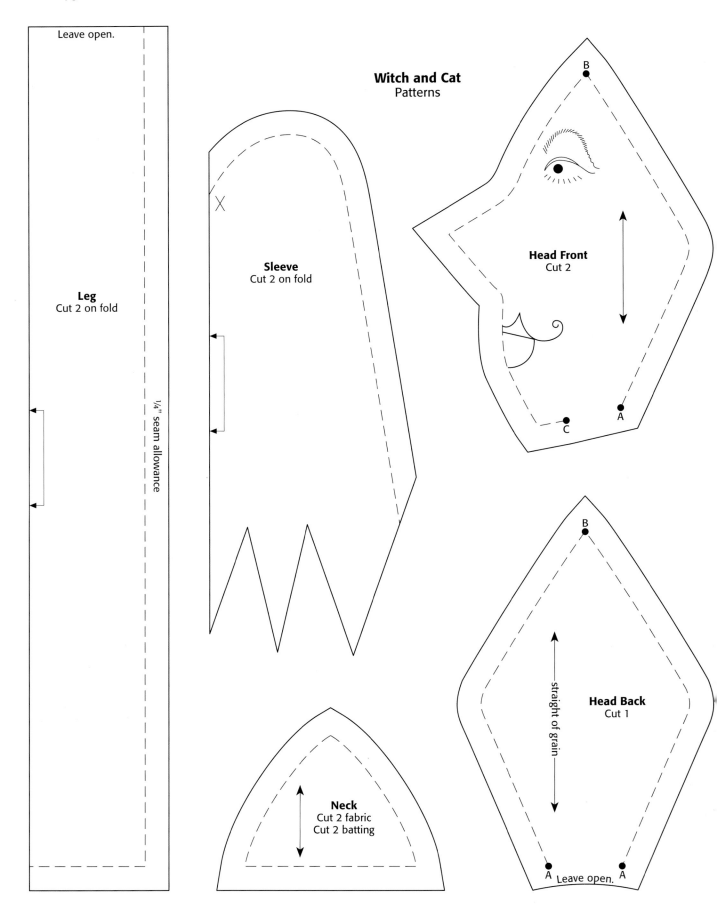

Leave open.

Leg
Cut 2 on fold

¼" seam allowance

Sleeve
Cut 2 on fold

Witch and Cat
Patterns

B

Head Front
Cut 2

C · · A

B

straight of grain

Head Back
Cut 1

A · Leave open. · A

Neck
Cut 2 fabric
Cut 2 batting

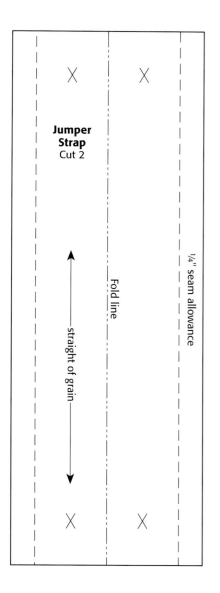

Jumper Strap
Cut 2

Fold line

straight of grain

¼" seam allowance

Witch and Cat
Patterns

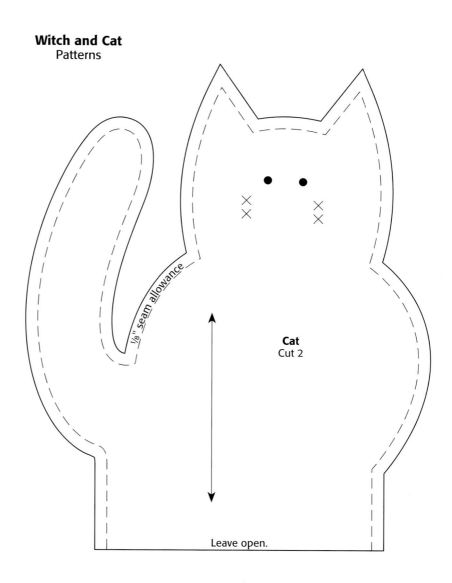

Cat
Cut 2

⅛" seam allowance

Leave open.

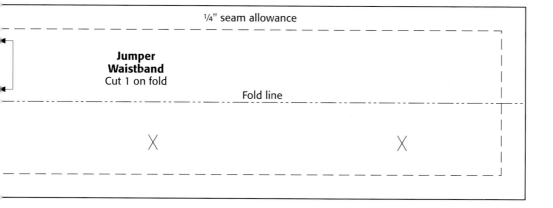

¼" seam allowance

Jumper Waistband
Cut 1 on fold

Fold line

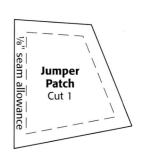

⅛" seam allowance

Jumper Patch
Cut 1

Witch and Cat
Patterns

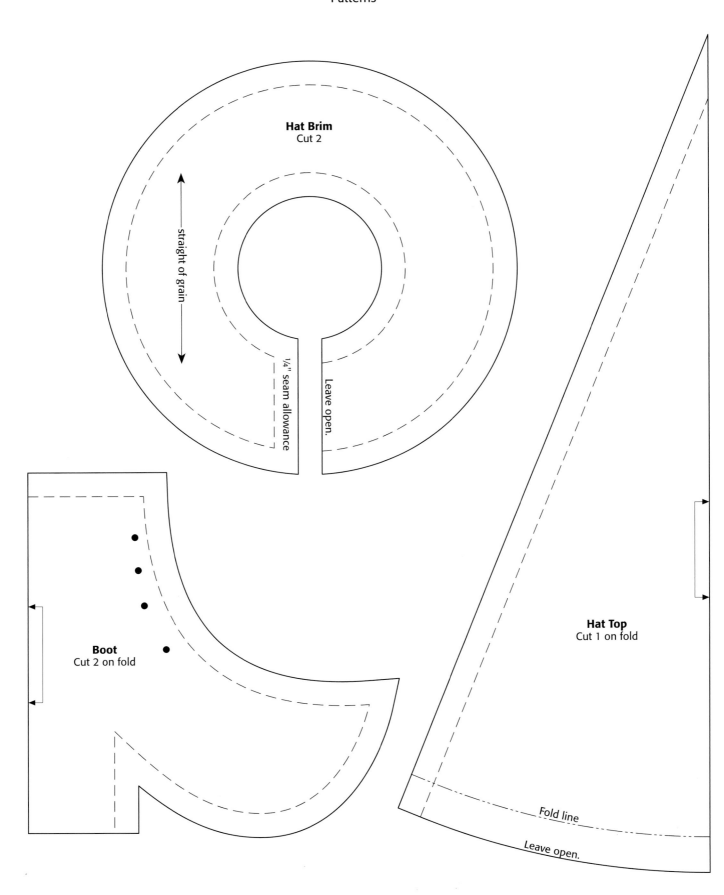

Hat Brim
Cut 2

straight of grain

1/4" seam allowance

Leave open.

Boot
Cut 2 on fold

Hat Top
Cut 1 on fold

Fold line

Leave open.

Crayon and Embroidery Wall Hanging
Patterns

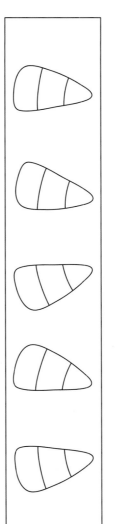

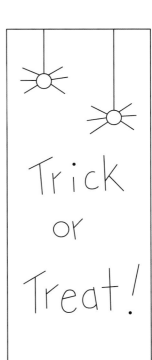

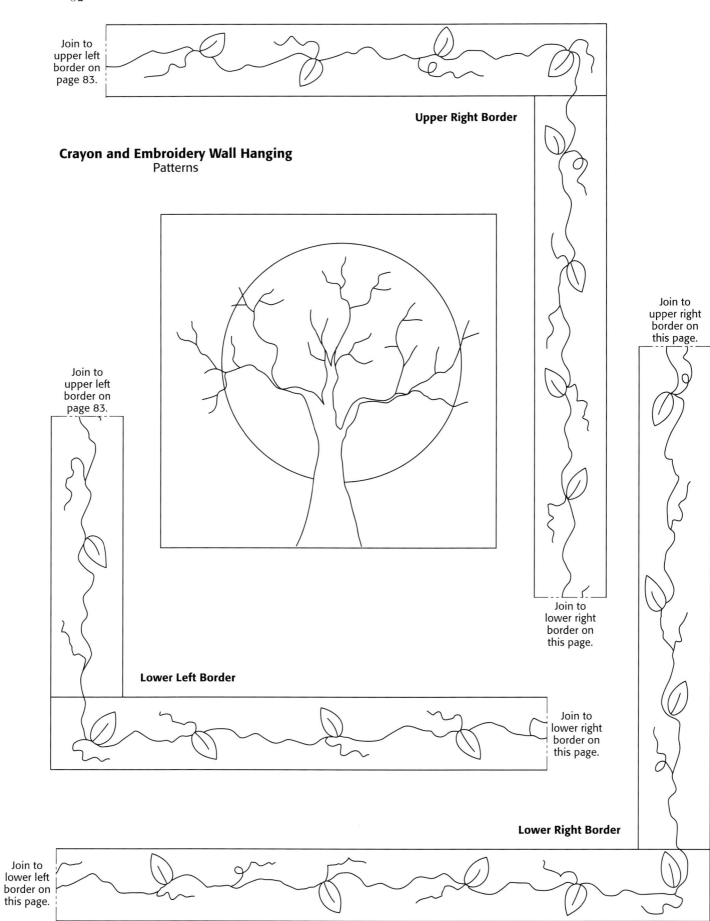

Join to upper left border on page 83.

Upper Right Border

Crayon and Embroidery Wall Hanging
Patterns

Join to upper right border on this page.

Join to upper left border on page 83.

Join to lower right border on this page.

Lower Left Border

Join to lower right border on this page.

Lower Right Border

Join to lower left border on this page.

Join to upper right border on page 82.

Upper Left Border

Crayon and Embroidery Wall Hanging
Patterns

Join to lower left border on page 82.

Haunted Birdhouse
Patterns

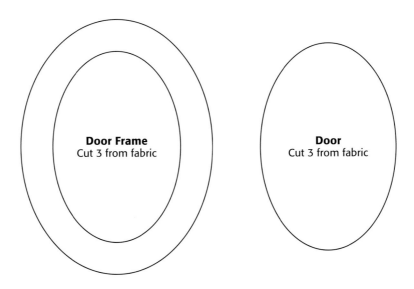

Door Frame
Cut 3 from fabric

Door
Cut 3 from fabric

**Chimney
Inside Wall**
Cut 1
from cardboard

Chimney Inside Wall
Cut 1 from fabric

Chimney Top
Cut 1 from fabric

Chimney Top
Cut 1
from cardboard

Haunted Birdhouse
Patterns

Shutter
Cut 6
from
cardboard

Shutter
Cut 3 and 3 reversed
from fabric

**Chimney
Side Wall**
Cut 1 and 1 reversed
from cardbord

**Chimney
Outside Wall**
Cut 1
from cardboard

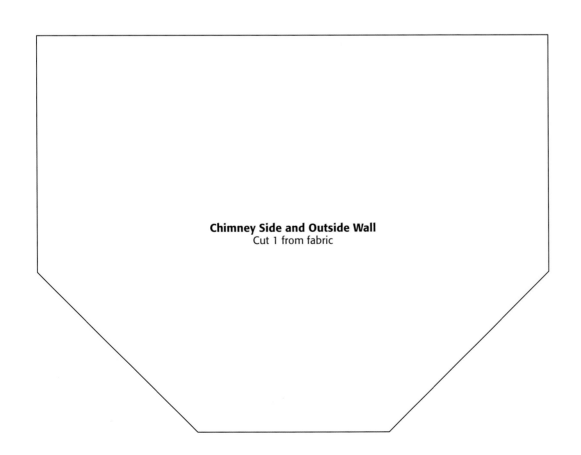

Chimney Side and Outside Wall
Cut 1 from fabric

86

Lanterns
Pumpkin Template

Lanterns
Black Cat Template

Ghost Treat Bags
Template

Ghost and Skeleton Luminaries
Patterns

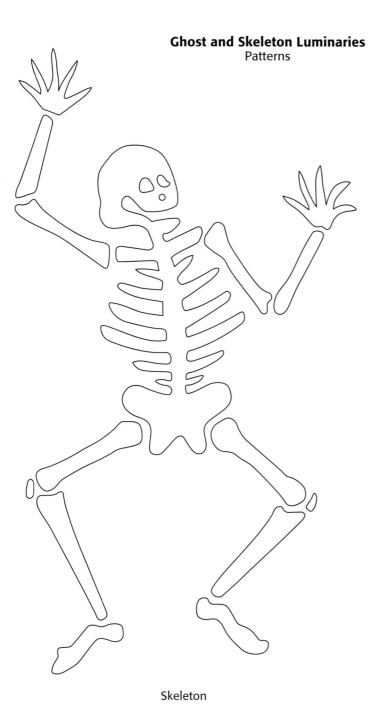

Skeleton

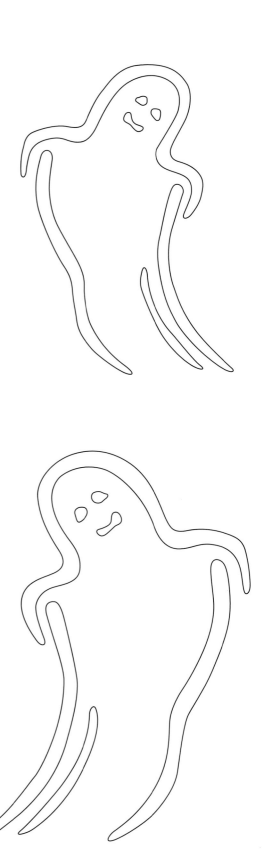

Ghosts

Painted Spiderweb Cake Plate
Template

Ghost Cake Dome
Templates

Appliquéd Pumpkin Table Runner
Patterns

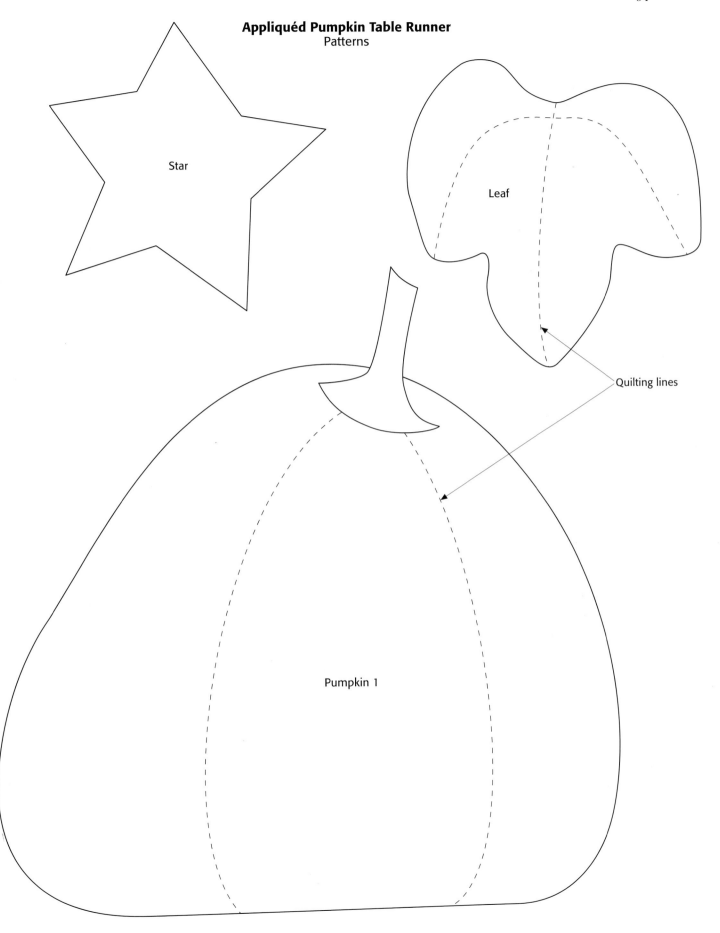

Star

Leaf

Quilting lines

Pumpkin 1

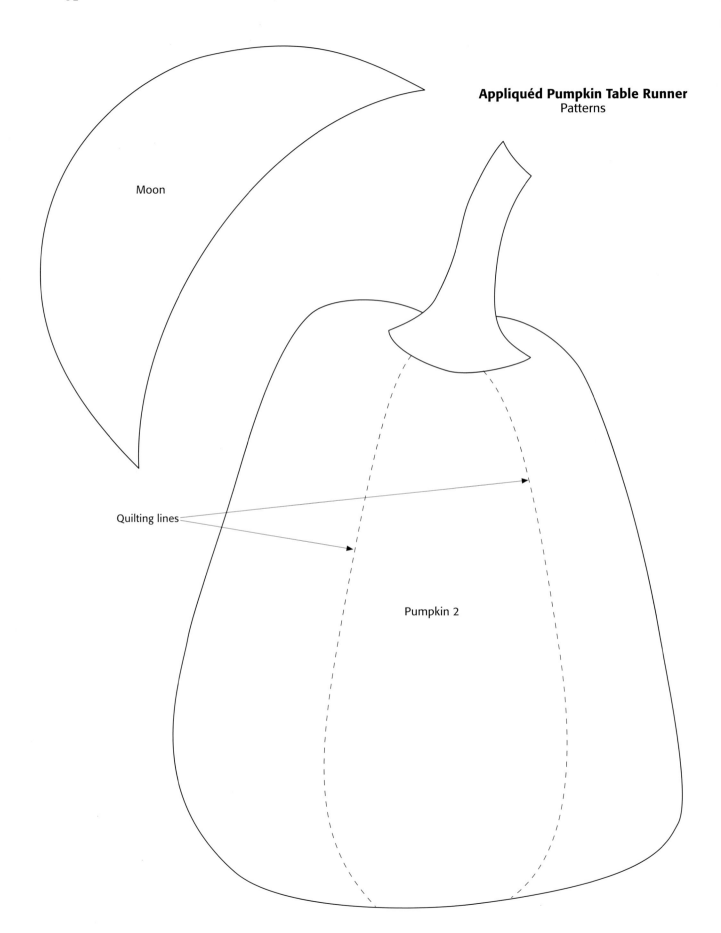

Appliquéd Pumpkin Table Runner
Patterns

Moon

Quilting lines

Pumpkin 2

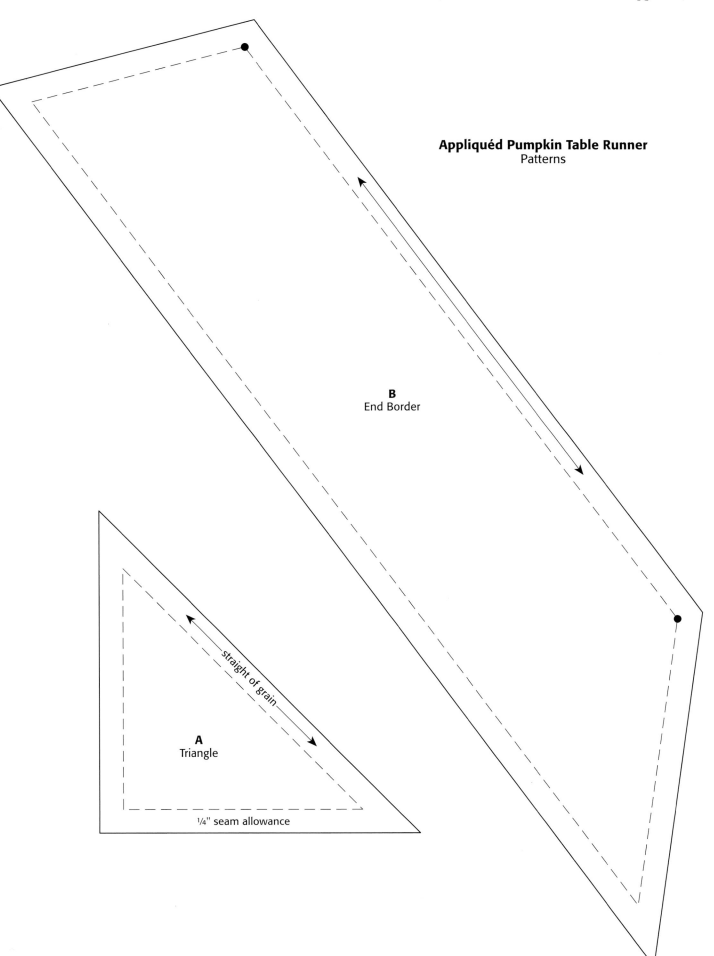

Appliquéd Pumpkin Table Runner
Patterns

B
End Border

straight of grain

A
Triangle

¼" seam allowance

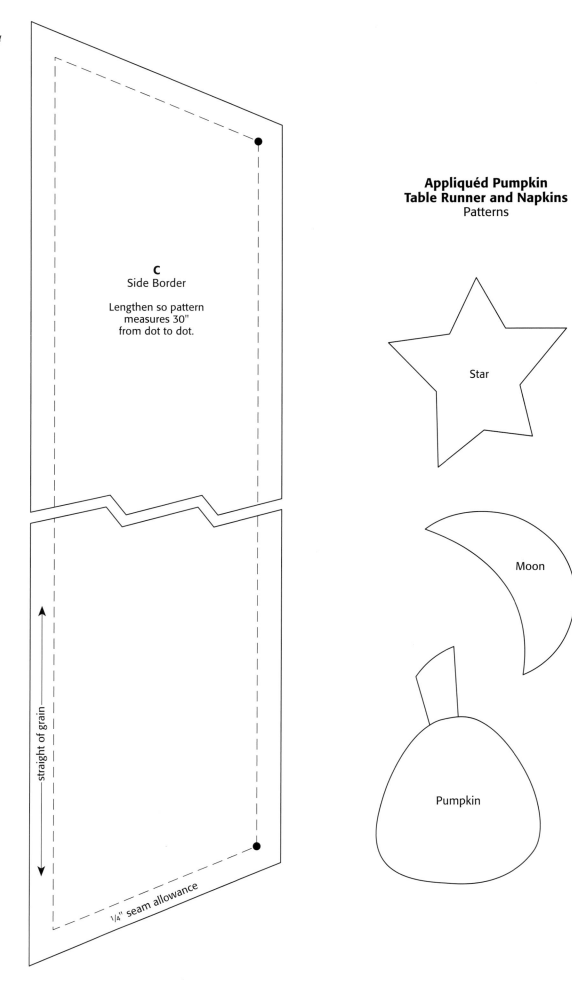

C
Side Border

Lengthen so pattern
measures 30"
from dot to dot.

straight of grain

¼" seam allowance

**Appliquéd Pumpkin
Table Runner and Napkins**
Patterns

Star

Moon

Pumpkin

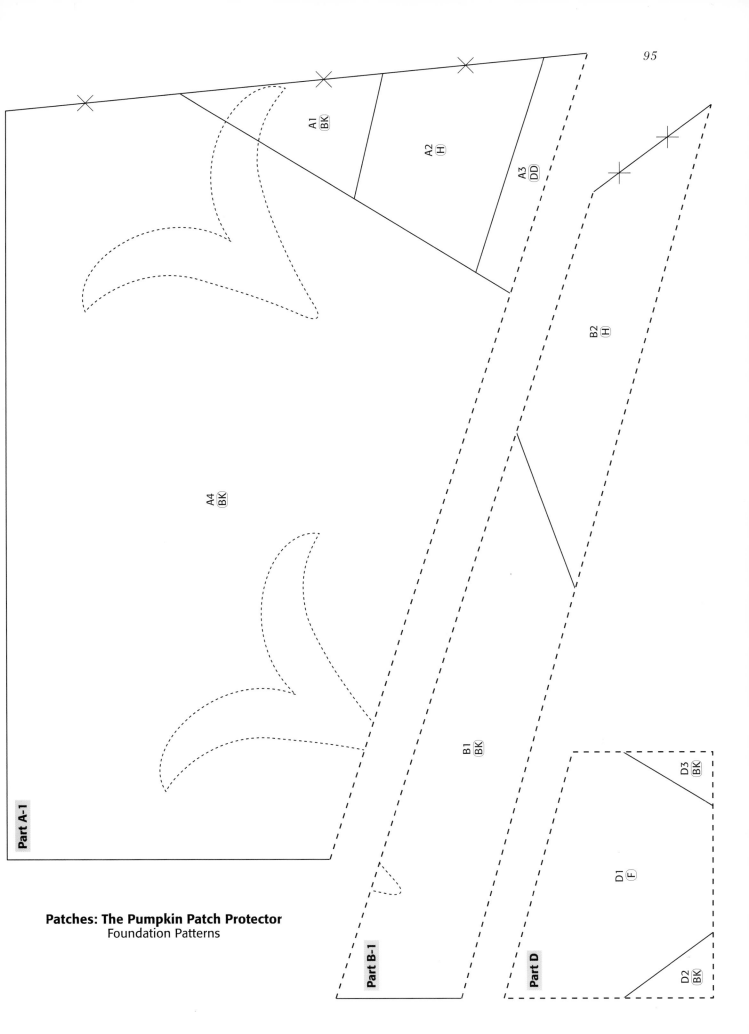

Patches: The Pumpkin Patch Protector
Foundation Patterns

Part A-1

A1
BK

A2
H

A3
DD

A4
BK

B2
H

B1
BK

Part B-1

Part D

D1
F

D2
BK

D3
BK

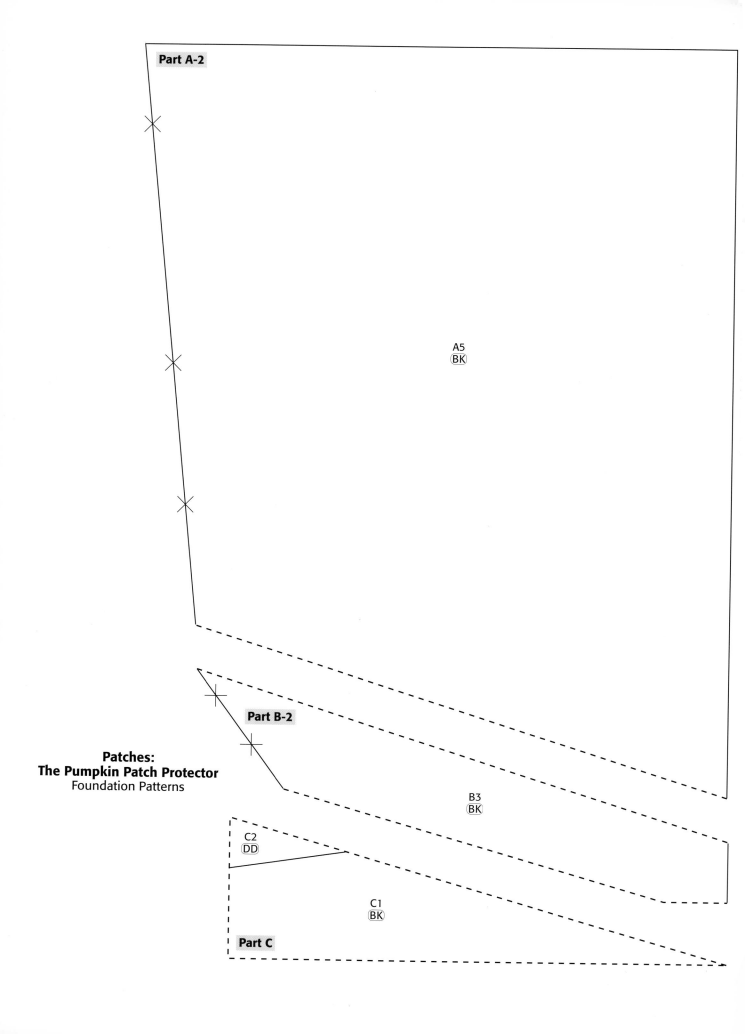

Part A-2

A5
(BK)

Part B-2

Patches:
The Pumpkin Patch Protector
Foundation Patterns

B3
(BK)

C2
(DD)

C1
(BK)

Part C

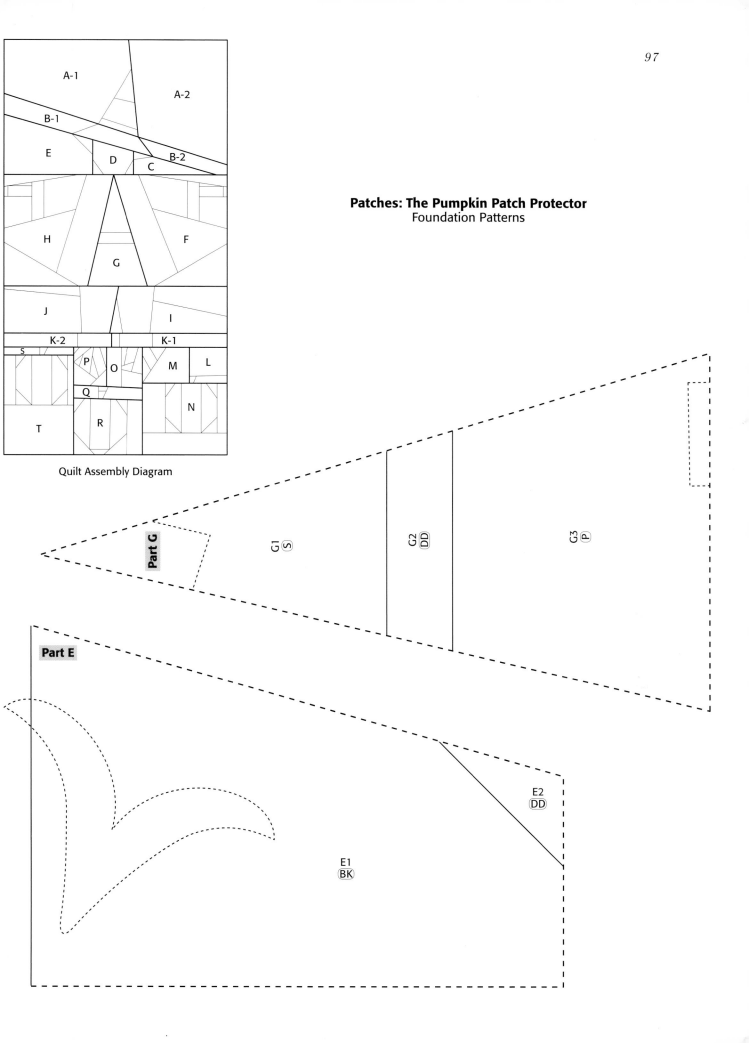

Patches: The Pumpkin Patch Protector
Foundation Patterns

Quilt Assembly Diagram

Part G

G1 Ⓢ

G2 ⒹⒹ

G3 Ⓟ

Part E

E2 ⒹⒹ

E1 Ⓑⓚ

Patches: The Pumpkin Patch Protector
Foundation Patterns

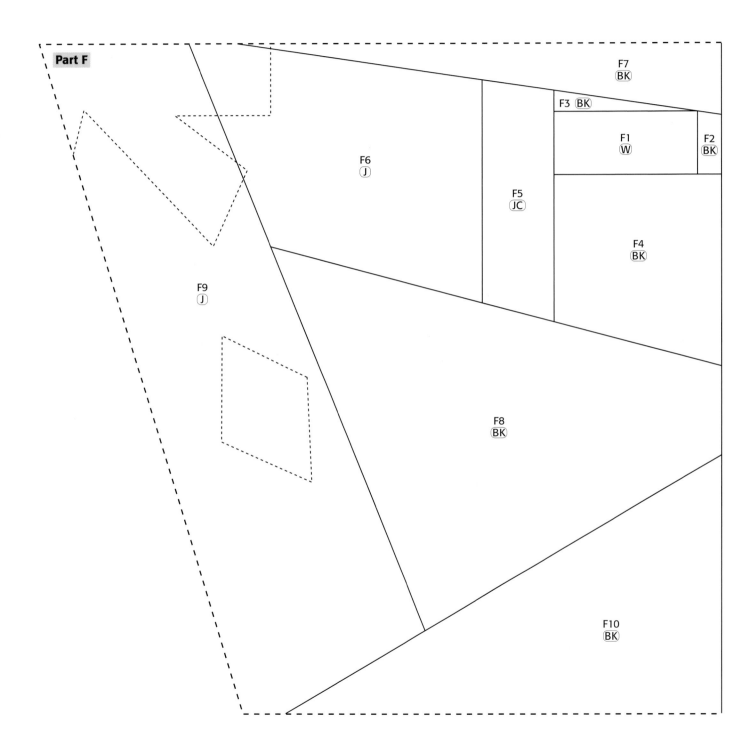

Patches: The Pumpkin Patch Protector
Foundation Patterns

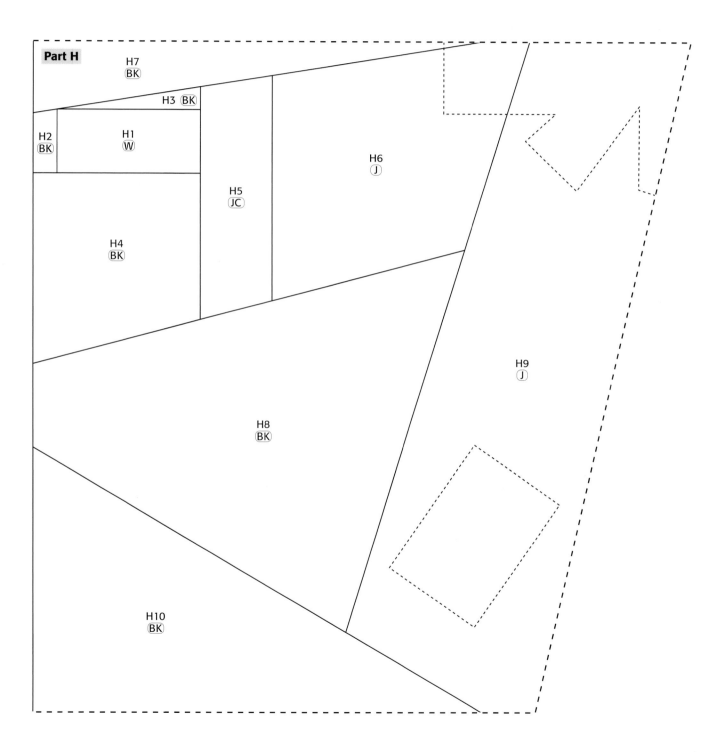

Patches: The Pumpkin Patch Protector
Foundation Patterns

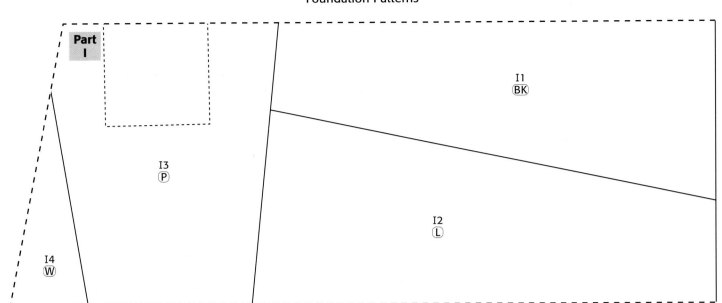

Part I

I1
(BK)

I3
(P)

I2
(L)

I4
(W)

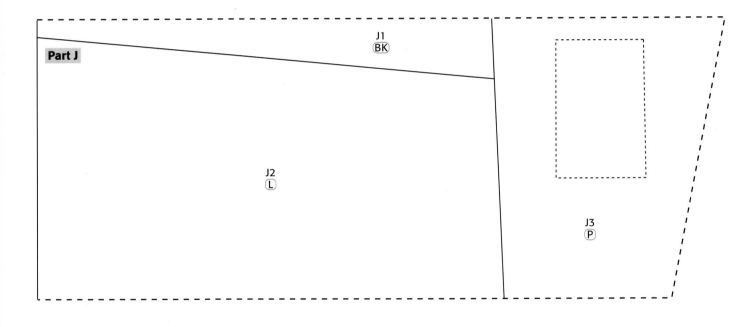

Part J

J1
(BK)

J2
(L)

J3
(P)

Part K-1

K3
(W)

K2
(PC)

K1
(L)

Part K-2

K5
(L)

K4
(PC)

Patches: The Pumpkin Patch Protector
Foundation Patterns

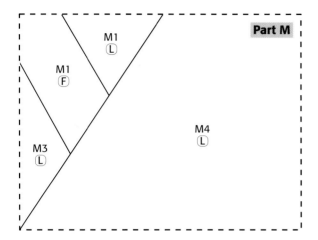

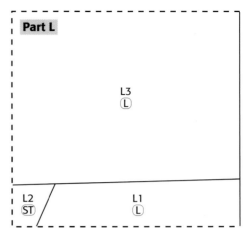

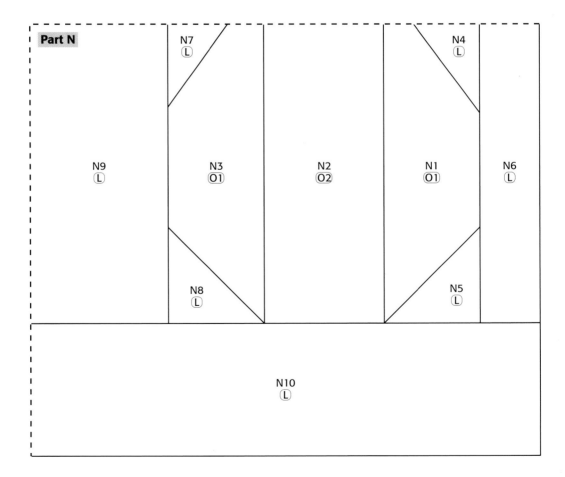

Patches: The Pumpkin Patch Protector
Foundation Patterns

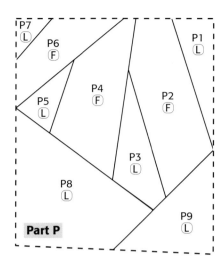

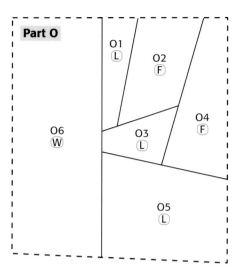

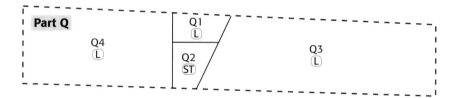

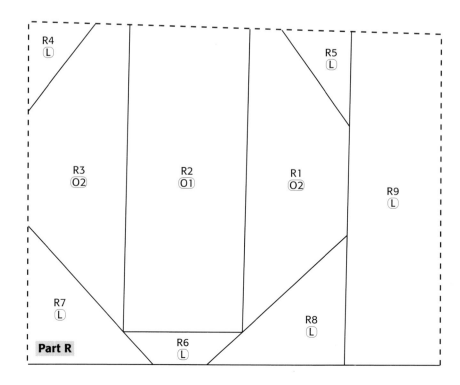

Patches: The Pumpkin Patch Protector
Foundation Patterns

Part S

| S3 (L) | S2 (ST) | S1 (L) |

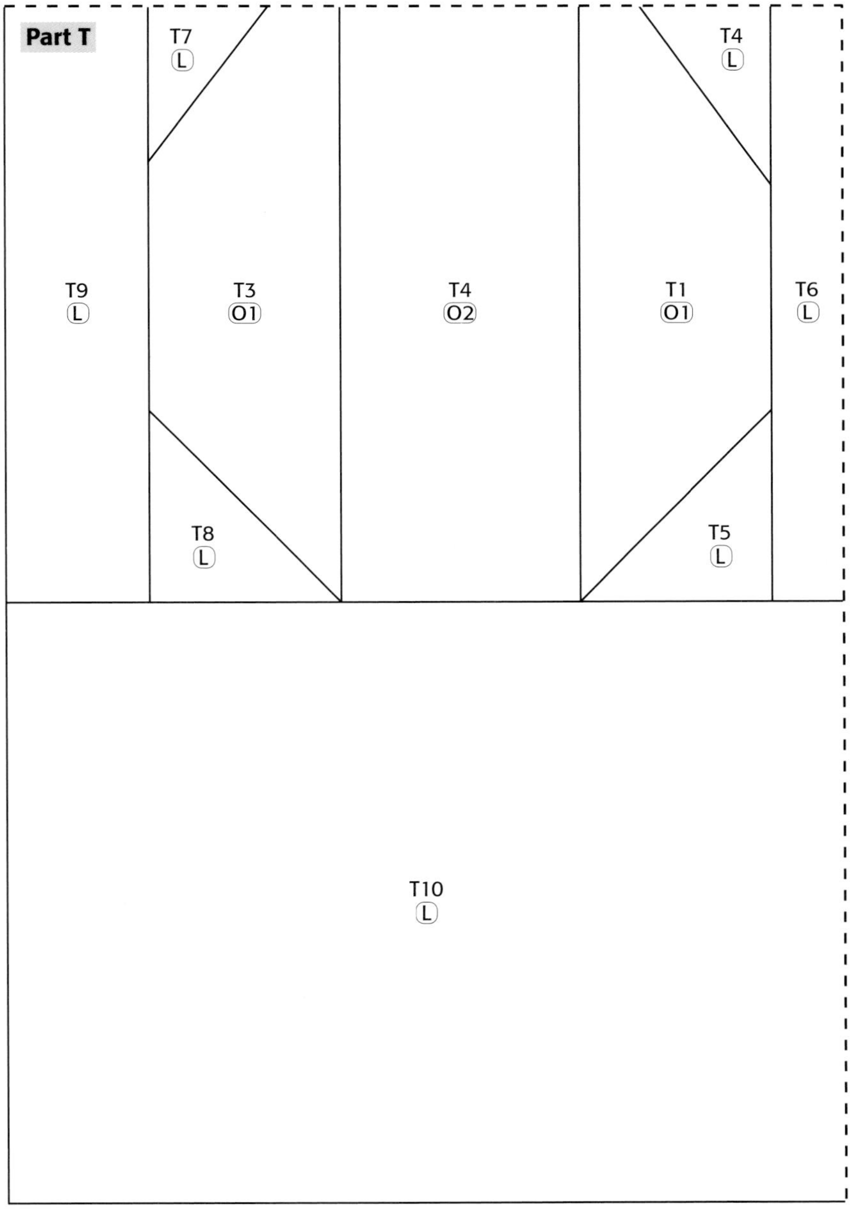

Part T

T7 (L)

T4 (L)

T9 (L) · T3 (O1) · T4 (O2) · T1 (O1) · T6 (L)

T8 (L)

T5 (L)

T10 (L)

Patches: The Pumpkin Patch Protector
Patterns

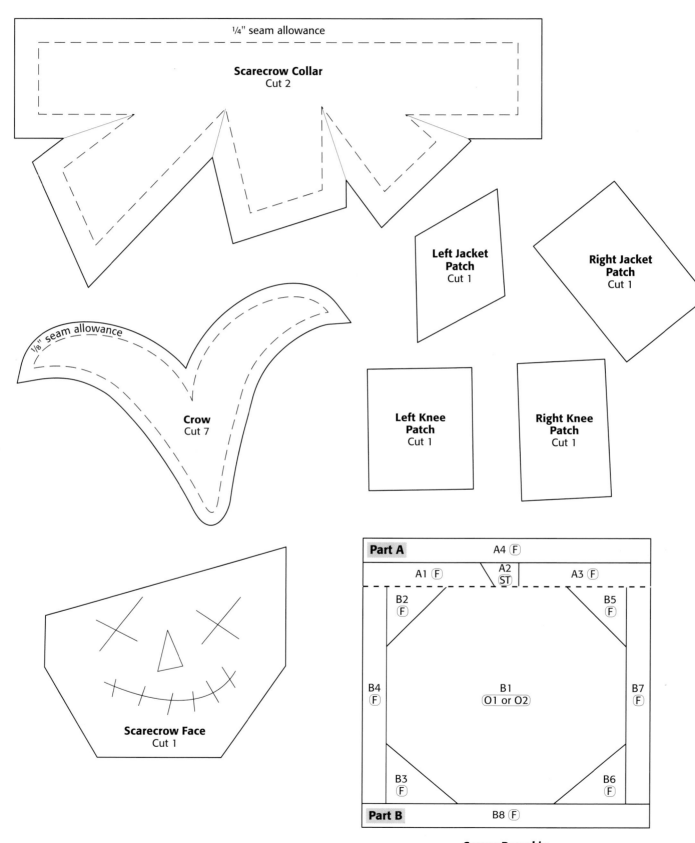

¼" seam allowance

Scarecrow Collar
Cut 2

⅛" seam allowance

Crow
Cut 7

Left Jacket Patch
Cut 1

Right Jacket Patch
Cut 1

Left Knee Patch
Cut 1

Right Knee Patch
Cut 1

Scarecrow Face
Cut 1

Part A   A4 (F)

A1 (F)   A2 (ST)   A3 (F)

B2 (F)   B5 (F)

B4 (F)   B1 (O1 or O2)   B7 (F)

B3 (F)   B6 (F)

Part B   B8 (F)

Corner Pumpkin
Foundation Pattern

Halloween Hooked Rugs
Scaredy Cat Pattern

Halloween Hooked Rugs
Happy Jack Pattern

Halloween Hooked Rugs
Boo! Pattern

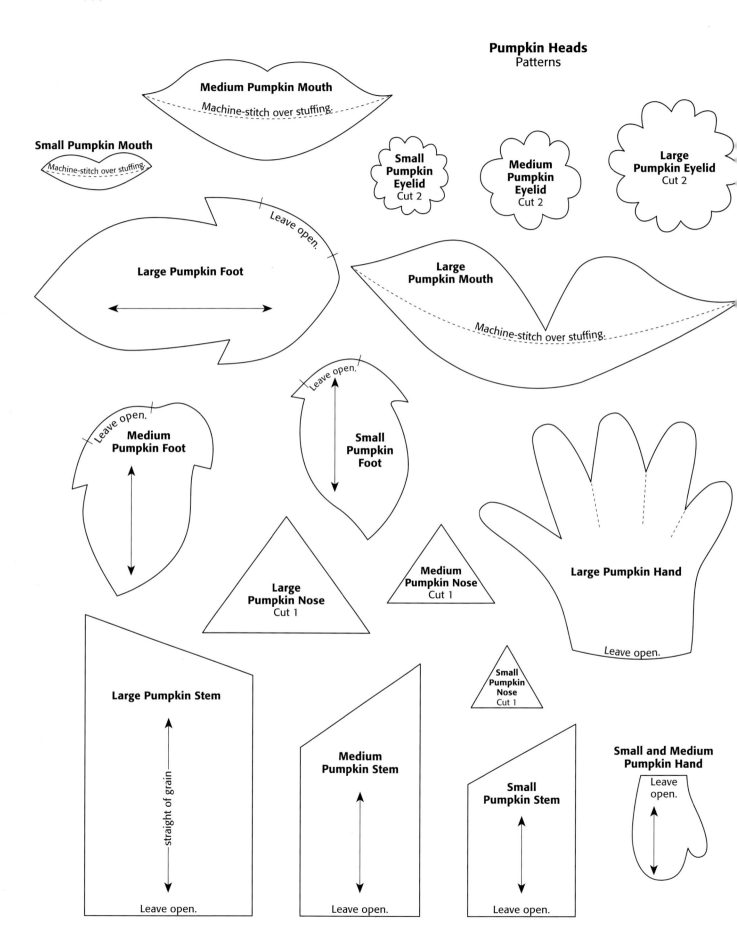

Pumpkin Heads
Patterns

Medium Pumpkin Mouth
Machine-stitch over stuffing.

Small Pumpkin Mouth
Machine-stitch over stuffing.

Small
Pumpkin
Eyelid
Cut 2

Medium
Pumpkin
Eyelid
Cut 2

Large
Pumpkin Eyelid
Cut 2

Leave open.

Large Pumpkin Foot

Large
Pumpkin Mouth

Machine-stitch over stuffing.

Leave open.

Medium
Pumpkin Foot

Leave open.

Small
Pumpkin
Foot

Large Pumpkin Hand

Large
Pumpkin Nose
Cut 1

Medium
Pumpkin Nose
Cut 1

Small
Pumpkin
Nose
Cut 1

Leave open.

Large Pumpkin Stem

straight of grain

Medium
Pumpkin Stem

Small
Pumpkin Stem

Small and Medium
Pumpkin Hand

Leave
open.

Leave open.

Leave open.

Leave open.

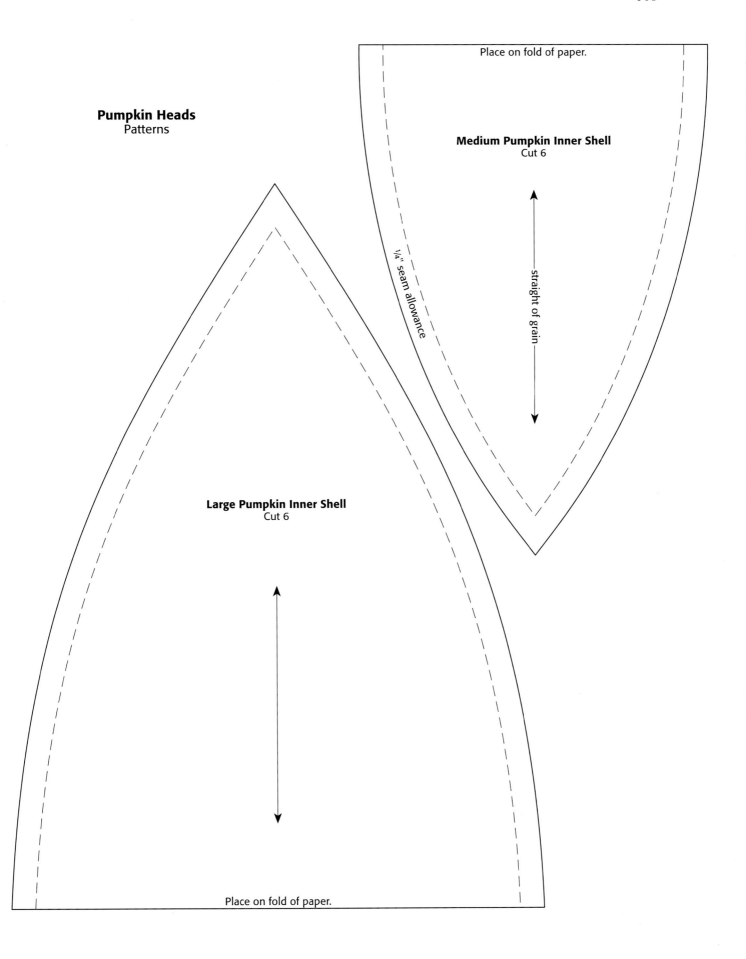

Pumpkin Heads
Patterns

Medium Pumpkin Inner Shell
Cut 6

Place on fold of paper.

¼" seam allowance

straight of grain

Large Pumpkin Inner Shell
Cut 6

Place on fold of paper.

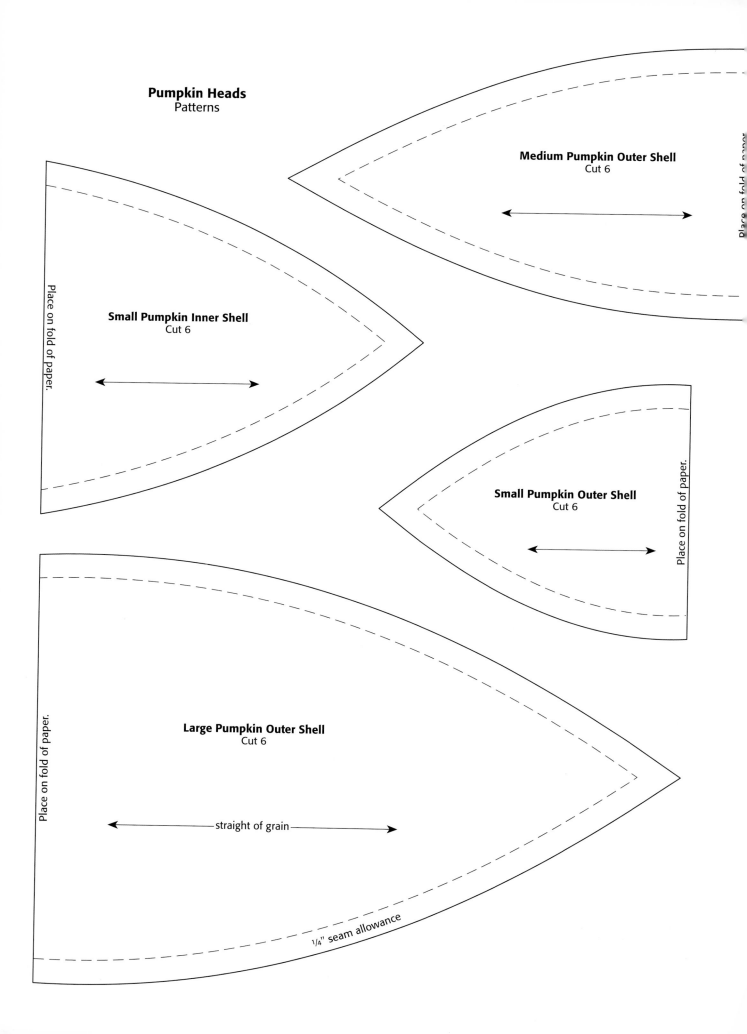

Pumpkin Heads
Patterns

Medium Pumpkin Outer Shell
Cut 6

Place on fold of paper.

Small Pumpkin Inner Shell
Cut 6

Place on fold of paper.

Small Pumpkin Outer Shell
Cut 6

Place on fold of paper.

Large Pumpkin Outer Shell
Cut 6

Place on fold of paper.

straight of grain

¼" seam allowance

Sources Guide

All Night Media, Inc.
PO Box 10607
San Rafael, CA 94912
800-782-6733
www.allnightmedia.com
Party Swirl Stamp

B & B Etching Products
18700 N. 107th Ave. #13
Sun City, AZ 85373-9759
888-382-4255
etchall@etchall.com
Stencils for glass etching, etching cream

Calico Moon Handcrafts
1919 State St.
Salem, OR 97301
800-678-7607
www.boxabilities.com
Cardboard birdhouse kits

Deka Paints
Box 309
Lamoille Industrial Park
Morrisville, VT 05661
800-532-7895
Deka Sign Enamel Paints, Clear Coat

Dover Publications
31 East 2nd Street
Mineola, NY 11501-3582
Publications, including 381 Old-Fashioned Holiday
Vignettes in Full Color *by Carol Belanger Grafton,
1993*

Impress
120 Andover Pk. E.
Tukwila, WA 98188
206-901-9101
*Cardstock, vellum, Anywhere hole punch eyelet
kits, glass-topped aluminum tins, Garamouche font*

Just Another Button Company
924 Wheat Ridge Drive
Troy, IL 62294
618-667-8531
Halloween buttons

Kunin Felt
380 Lafayette Road
PO Box 5000
Hamton, NH 03843-5000
800-292-7900
www.kuninfelt.com
Kreative Kanvas

Martingale & Company
PO Box 118
Bothell, WA 98041-0118
800-426-3126
www.patchwork.com
Photo transfer paper

Moondance Color Co.
622 Spencer Rd.
Oakham, MA 01068
508-882-3383
www.moondancecolor.com
Hand-dyed wool for rug hooking

New Earth Designs
81 Lake Rd.
Brookfield, MA 01506
508-867-8114
email: newearthdesigns@juno.com
Hand-dyed wool for rug hooking

Pourette Mfg. Co.
P.O. Box 17056
Seattle, WA 98107
800-888-9425
Candle mold, candlemaking supplies

Pumpkin Masters, Inc.
P.O. Box 61456
Denver, CO 80206
www.pumpkinmasters.com
Pumpkin carving tools

Rubbermoon
12670 Strahorn Rd.
Hayden Lake, ID 83835
208-772-9772
Rubber Stamps

Contributor:
Midori Inc.
708-6th Avenue North
Seattle, WA 98109
206-282-3595
18"-wide Sinamay Ribbon

Martingale & Company
Toll-free: 1-800-426-3126

International: 1-425-483-3313
24-Hour Fax: 1-425-486-7596

PO Box 118, Bothell, WA 98041-0118 USA

Web site: www.patchwork.com
E-mail: info@martingale-pub.com

Books from

These books are available through your local quilt, fabric, craft-supply, or art-supply store. For more information, contact us for a free full-color catalog. You can also find our full catalog of books online at www.patchwork.com.

1/00